BERLITZ® Books
for travellers

TRAVEL GUIDES

They fit your pocket in both size and price. Modern, up-to-date, Berlitz gets all the information you need into 128 lively pages with colour maps and photos throughout. What to see and do, where to shop, what to eat and drink, how to save.

TRAVEL GUIDES

AFRICA	Kenya
	South Africa
ASIA, MIDDLE EAST	China (256 pages)
	Hong Kong
	Singapore
	Sri Lanka
	Thailand
	Egypt
	Morocco
	Tunisia
	Jerusalem and the Holy Land
BRITISH ISLES	London
	Ireland
	Oxford and Stratford
	Scotland
BELGIUM	Brussels
FRANCE	French Riviera
	Loire Valley
	Paris

PHRASE BOOKS

World's bestselling phrase books feature all the expressions and vocabulary you'll need, and pronunciation throughout. 192 pages, 2 colours.

Arabic
Chinese
Danish
Dutch
Finnish
French
German
Greek
Hebrew
Hungarian
Italian
Japanese

Norwegian
Polish
Portuguese
Russian
Serbo-Croatian
Spanish (Castilian)
Spanish (Lat. Am.)
Swahili
Swedish
Turkish
European Phrase Book
European Menu Reader

GERMANY	Berlin Munich The Rhine Valley		**SPAIN**	Barcelona and Costa Dorada Canary Islands Costa Blanca Costa Brava Costa del Sol and Andalusia Ibiza and Formentera Madrid Majorca and Minorca
AUSTRIA and SWITZER-LAND	Austrian Tyrol Vienna Geneva / French-speaking areas Zurich / German-speaking areas			
			EASTERN EUROPE	Budapest Dubrovnik and Southern Dalmatia Hungary (192 pages) Istria and Croatian Coast Moscow Split and Dalmatia
GREECE	Athens Corfu Crete Rhodes Greek Islands of the Aegean Salonica and Northern Greece			
			NORTH AMERICA	U.S.A. (256 pages) California Florida Hawaii Montreal New York
ITALY and MALTA	Florence Italian Adriatic Italian Riviera Rome Sicily Venice Malta			
			CARIBBEAN, LATIN AMERICA	Puerto Rico Virgin Islands Bahamas Bermuda French West Indies Jamaica Southern Caribbean Mexico City Rio de Janeiro
NETHER-LANDS and SCANDI-NAVIA	Amsterdam Copenhagen Helsinki Oslo and Bergen Stockholm			
			EUROPE	Business Travel Guide – Europe (368 pages)

Most titles with British and U.S. destinations are available
in French, German, Spanish and as many as 7 other languages.

BERLITZ

german
english
englisch
deutsch

DICTIONARIES

Bilingual with 12,500 concepts each way.
Highly practical for travellers, with
pronunciation shown plus menu reader, basic
expressions and useful information.
Over 330 pages.

Danish	Italian
Dutch	Norwegian
Finnish	Portuguese
French	Spanish
German	Swedish

**Berlitz Books, a world of information in your pocket!
At all leading bookshops and airport newsstands.**

Take this 30-lesson BERLITZ® home study course and make your trip even more enjoyable!

With a few foreign words, your trip (and you) can be more interesting. Enjoy the satisfaction of knowing a new language, meeting people, getting involved?

Now you can learn – easily, painlessly – without leaving your home. Berlitz, the company whose name is synonymous with language instruction has a basic Cassette Course for you in French, German, Italian or Spanish.

Here's what your Berlitz Cassette Course brings you...

1. 90-minute "zero" or beginner's cassette with 10 basic lessons.

2. Two 60-minute cassettes – 20 more lessons in all, on what to say when abroad.

3. Two illustrated books featuring the text of all cassettes with explanatory notes, instructions for easy reference.

4. Unique rotating verb finder showing tenses of all key verbs.

5. As an extra bonus, a Berlitz phrase book plus a pocket dictionary for any emergency.

There are thirty lively lessons in all – three and one-half hours of playing (and replaying) time. No grammar – not until you're ready. Just listen and repeat at your own pace – in the privacy of your own home.

 Dial (no charge) 24 hours, 7 days a week.

In the U.S.A.

1-800-223-1814

(New York Residents Dial 212-944-9300).

In Great Britain

0323-638221

Refer to Dept. No. 11576. Why not give us a ring – right now!

Treat yourself to an hour with BERLITZ®

Just listen and repeat

It's fun, not work. And you'll surprise your friends and yourself: it's so easy to pick up some basic expressions in the foreign language of your choice. These cassettes are recorded in hi-fi with four voices. Bringing native speakers into your home, they permit you to improve your accent and learn the basic phrases before you depart.

With each cassette is a helpful 32-page script, containing pronunciation tips, plus complete text of the dual-language recording.

An ideal companion for your Berlitz phrase book, pocket dictionary or travel guide. Order now!

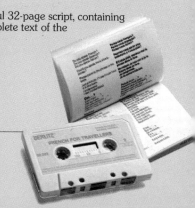

$9.95/£5.95 (incl. VAT)
use convenient envelope attached.

Treat yourself to an hour with Berlitz

Just listen and repeat

It's fun, not work. And you'll surprise your friends and yourself with the speed you pick up some basic expressions in the foreign language of your choice. These cassettes are recorded in hi-fi with four voices. Bringing native speakers into your home, they permit you to polish your accent and learn the basic phrases before you depart.

With each cassette is a helpful 32-page script, containing pronunciation tips and the complete text of the dual-language recording.

An ideal companion for your Berlitz phrase book, pocket dictionary or travel guide. Order now!

BERLITZ SINGLE CASSETTES
Only $9.95/£5.95 (incl. VAT)

Arabic	218 ☐	Italian	206 ☐
Chinese	221 ☐	Japanese	207 ☐
Danish	200 ☐	Norwegian	208 ☐
Dutch	212 ☐	Portuguese	214 ☐
Finnish	201 ☐	Russian	209 ☐
French	202 ☐	Serbo-Croatian	215 ☐
German	203 ☐	Spanish (Castil)	210 ☐
Greek	204 ☐	Spanish (Lat Am)	213 ☐
Hebrew	205 ☐	Swedish	211 ☐

TOTAL SINGLES [____]

Please note the total number of each item requested and complete the reverse side of this order form. **11405**

BERLITZ®

SWEDISH
FOR TRAVELLERS

By the staff of Editions Berlitz

Library of Congress Catalog Card Number: 75-11286

Revised edition
8th printing 1984

Printed in Switzerland

Berlitz Trademark Reg. U.S. Patent Office
and other countries—Marca Registrada

Editions Berlitz
1, avenue des Jordils
1000 Lausanne 6, Switzerland

Preface

In preparing this complete revision of *Swedish for Travellers,* we have taken into consideration a wealth of suggestions and criticisms from phrase-book users around the world. As a result, this new edition features:

a) a complete phonetic transcription throughout indicating the pronunciation of all words and phrases you'll need to know on your trip

b) special sections showing the replies your listener might give to you. Just hand him the book and let him point to the appropriate phrase. This is especially practical in certain difficult situations (doctor, garage mechanic, etc.).

c) a complete revision of the section on Eating Out to make it even more useful in a restaurant

d) a tipping chart and a more comprehensive reference section in the back of the book.

These are new features. They complement what has become the world's most popular phrase-book series, helping you with:

* all the phrases and supplementary vocabulary you'll need on your trip

* a wide variety of tourist and travel facts, tips and useful information

* quick reference through colour coding. The major features of the contents are on the back cover. A complete index is found inside.

These are just a few of the practical advantages. In addition, the book will prove a valuable introduction to life in Sweden.

There's a comprehensive section on Eating Out, giving translations and explanations for practically anything one would find on a Swedish menu; there's a complete Shopping Guide that will enable you to obtain virtually anything you want. Trouble with the car? Turn to the mechanic's manual with its dual-language terms. Feeling ill? Our medical section provides the most rapid communication possible between you and the doctor.

To make the most of *Swedish for Travellers,* we suggest that you start with the "Guide to pronunciation". Then go on to "Some basic expressions". This not only gives you a minimum vocabulary; it helps you to pronounce the language.

We're particularly grateful to Miss Inger Eriksson, Mrs. Catherine Nerfin and Mr. David Pulman for their help in the preparation of this book and to Dr. T.J.A. Bennett who devised the phonetic transcription. We also wish to thank the Swedish National Travel Office for its assistance.

We shall be very pleased to receive any comments, criticisms and suggestions that you think may help us in preparing future editions.

Thank you. Have a good trip.

Throughout this book, the symbols illustrated here indicate small sections where phrases have been compiled that your foreign listener might like to say to *you*. If you don't understand him, give him the book and let him point to the phrase in his language. The English translation is just beside it.

Basic grammar

Here is the briefest possible outline of some essential features of Swedish grammar.

Articles

All Swedish nouns are either common or neuter in gender.

1. Indefinite article (a/an)

common:	**en man**	a man
neuter:	**ett barn**	a child

2. Definite article (the)

common:	**mannen**	the man
neuter:	**barnet**	the child

Plural: see "Nouns".

Nouns

1. As already noted, nouns are either common or neuter. There are no easy rules for determining gender. Learn each new word with its accompanying article.

2. Nouns form their plurals according to one of five declensions.

		singular		indefinite plurals	
Declension	1	**flicka**	girl	**flickor**	girls
	2	**bil**	car	**bilar**	cars
	3	**dam**	lady	**damer**	ladies
	4	**äpple**	apple	**äpplen**	apples
	5	**hus**	house	**hus**	houses

		definite plurals	
common:		**flickorna**	the girls
neuter:		**husen**	the houses

There are also various irregular plurals.

3. Possession is shown by adding **-s** (singular and plural). *Note:* There is no apostrophe.

Görans bror	George's brother
hotellets ägare	the owner of the hotel
veckans första dag	the first day of the week
den resandes väska	the traveller's suitcase
barnens rum	the children's room

Adjectives

1. Adjectives agree with the noun in gender and number. For the indefinite form, the neuter is formed by adding **-t**; the plural by adding **-a.**

en stor hund	a big dog	**stora hundar**	big dogs
ett stort hus	a big house	**stora hus**	big houses

2. For the definite declension of the adjective, add the ending **-a** (common, neuter and plural). This form is used when the adjective is preceded by **den, det, de** (the definite article used with adjectives) or by a demonstrative adjective.

en svensk bil	a Swedish car
den svenska bilen	the Swedish car
de svenska bilarna	the Swedish cars
ett stort hus	a big house
det stora huset	the big house
de stora husen	the big houses

3. **Demonstrative adjectives:**

	common	neuter	plural
this/these	**den här/ denna**	**det här/ detta**	**de här/ dessa**
that/those	**den där/ den**	**det där/ det**	**de där/ de**

4. Possessive adjectives:

	common	neuter	plural
my	min	mitt	mina
your*	din	ditt	dina
our	vår	vårt	våra
your*	er	ert	era

All the above agree with the noun they modify.

	common	neuter	plural
his	hans	hans	hans
her	hennes	hennes	hennes
its	dess	dess	dess
their	deras	deras	deras

These are indeclinable.

The comparative and superlative are normally formed either by adding the endings **-(a)re** and **-(a)st**, respectively, to the adjective or by adding **mer** and **mest**, respectively, before the adjective.

Er bil är stor.	Your car is big.
Er bil är större.	Your car is bigger.
Er bil är störst.	Your car is the biggest.
Hans arbete är intressant.	His work is interesting.
Hans arbete är intressantare.	His work is more interesting.
Hans arbete är intressantast.	His work is the most interesting.

Adverbs

Adverbs are generally formed by adding **-t** to the corresponding adjective.

Hon går snabbt.	She walks quickly.

* see page 10 under "Personal pronouns"

Personal pronouns

	subject	object
I	jag	mig
you	du	dig
he	han	honom
she	hon	henne
it	den/det	den/det
we	vi	oss
you	ni	er
they	de	dem

Like many other languages, Swedish has two forms for
"you". The formal word **ni**, traditionally the correct form
of address between all but close friends and children, is
now giving way to the informal **du**.

Verbs

Here we are concerned only with the infinitive, impera-
tive, and present tense. The present tense is simple,
because it has the same form for all persons. The infinitive
of most Swedish verbs ends in **-a** (a few verbs of one
syllable end in other vowels). The present tense ends
in **-r**:

	to be	to have	to be able to
Infinitive	**(att) vara**	**(att) ha**	**(att) kunna**
Present tense (same form for all persons)	**är**	**har**	**kan**
Imperative	**var**	**ha**	**–**

GRAMMAR

	to ask	to buy	to believe
Infinitive	**(att) fråga**	**(att) köpa**	**(att) tro**
Present tense (same form for all persons)	**frågar**	**köper**	**tror**
Imperative	**fråga**	**köp**	**tro**

There is no equivalent to the English present continuous tense. Thus:

Jag reser.	I travel/I am travelling.

Negatives

Negation is expressed by using the adverb **inte** (not). It is usually placed immediately after the verb in a main clause. In compound tenses **inte** comes between the auxiliary and the main verb.

Jag talar svenska.	I speak Swedish.
Jag talar inte svenska.	I do not speak Swedish.
Hon har inte skrivit.	She has not written.

Questions

Questions are formed by reversing the order of the subject and the verb:

Jag kommer i kväll.	I am coming tonight.
Kommer ni i kväll?	Are you coming tonight?

There is/There are

Det finns många turister.	There are many tourists.

It is

Det är varmt idag.	It is warm today.

Guide to pronunciation

This and the following chapter are intended to make you familiar with the phonetic transcription we have devised and to help you get used to the sounds of Swedish.

As a minimum vocabulary for your trip, we've selected a number of basic words and phrases under the title "Some basic expressions" (pages 16-21).

An outline of the spelling and sounds of Swedish

You'll find the pronunciation of the Swedish letters and sounds explained below, as well as the symbols we're using for them in the transcriptions. The imitated pronunciation should be read as if it were English except for any special rules set out below. If you follow carefully the indications supplied here, you'll have no difficulty in reading our transcriptions in such a way as to make yourself understood. Syllables printed in **bold type** should be stressed. A bar over part of a word (sha̅yf) in the phonetic transcription indicates a long vowel.

Consonants

Letter	Approximate pronunciation	Symbol	Example	
b, c, d, f, h, l, m, n, p, v, w, x	as in English			
ch	at the beginning of words borrowed from French, like **sh** in **sh**ut	sh	**chef**	sha̅yf
g	1) before stressed **i, e, y, ä, ö** and sometimes after **l** or **r**, like **y** in yet	y	**get**	ya̅yt

	2) before **e** and **i** in many words of French origin, like **sh** in **sh**ut	sh	**generös**	sh$\overline{ay}$nerr**u**̄rss
	3) elsewhere, generally like **g** in go	g	**gaffel**	**g**ahferl
j, dj, **gj, lj**	like **y** in **y**et	y	**ja**	yaa
k	1) before stressed **i, e, y, ä, ö,** generally like **ch** in Scottish lo**ch**, but pronounced in the front of the mouth	kh	**köpa**	kh$\overline{u}$rpah
	2) elsewhere, like **k** in **k**it	k	**klippa**	**k**lippah
kj	like **ch** in Scottish lo**ch**, but pronounced in the front of the mouth	kh	**kjol**	kh$\overline{oo}$l
qu	like **k** in **k**it followed by **v** in **v**at	kv	**Lindquist**	lind**k**vist
r	slightly rolled near the front of the mouth	r	**ryka**	r$\overline{ew}$kah
s	1) in the ending **-sion** like **sh** in **sh**ut	sh	**mission**	mish$\overline{oo}$n
	2) elsewhere, like **s** in **s**o	s/ss	**ses**	s$\overline{ay}$ss
	3) the groups **sch, skj, stj** are pronounced like **sh** in **sh**ut	sh	**schema**	**sh**$\overline{ay}$mah
sk	1) before stressed **e, i, y, ä, ö,** like **sh** in **sh**ut	sh	**skänk**	shehnk
	2) elsewhere, like **sk** in **sk**ip	sk	**skola**	**sk**$\overline{oo}$la
t	1) **ti** in the ending **-tion** pronounced like **sh** in **sh**ut or like **ch** in **ch**at	sh	**station**	stah**sh**$\overline{oo}$n
		tsh	**nation**	naht**sh**$\overline{oo}$n
	2) elsewhere, like **t** in **t**op	t	**tid**	teed
tj	like **ch** in Scottish lo**ch**, but pronounced in the front of the mouth; sometimes with a **t**-sound at the beginning	kh	**tjäna**	**kh**ainah
z	like **s** in **s**o	s	**zenit**	s$\overline{ay}$nit

N.B. In the groups **rd, rl, rn, rs** and **rt**, the letter **r** is generally not pronounced but influences the pronunciation of the following consonant which is then pronounced with the tip of the tongue *not* on the upper front teeth, but behind the gums of the upper teeth. We indicate this pronunciation of **d, l, n, s** or **t** by printing a small **r** above the line, e.g. *svart* is pronounced svah^{r}t.

Vowels

A vowel is generally long in stressed syllables when it's the final letter or followed by only one consonant. If followed by two or more consonants or in unstressed syllables, the vowel is generally short.

a	1) when long, like **a** in car	aa	**dag**	daag
	2) when short, something like the **u** in cut or **o** in American college	ah	**tack**	tahk
e	1) when long, like **ay** in say, but a *pure* vowel, not a diphthong	a͞y	**sen**	sa͞yn
	2) in the stressed prefix **er-**, like **a** in man, but longer	æ	**erfara**	ǣrfaarah
	3) when short, like **e** in get	eh	**beck**	behk
	4) when unstressed, like **a** in about	er*	**betala**	bertaalah
ej	like **a** in mate	ay	**nej**	nay
i	1) when long, like **ee** in bee	ee	**vit**	veet
	2) when short, between **ee** in meet and **i** in hit	i	**hinna**	hinnah
	3) in a few words, e.g. in the personal pronoun **mig,** like **a** in mate	ay	**mig**	may
o	1) when long, often like **oo** in soon, but with the lips more tightly rounded, and with a puff of breath at the end	o͞o	**sko**	sko͞o
	2) the same sound can be short	oo	**solid**	sooleed
	3) when long, it is also sometimes pronounced like **oa** in moan but a pure vowel	oa	**son**	soan
	4) when short, sometimes like **o** in hot	o	**korrekt**	korrehkt
u	1) when long, like Swedish **y,** but with the tongue a little lower in the mouth, and with a puff of breath at the end; you'll find it very hard to distinguish from Swedish **y,** so we'll use the same symbol for both	e͞w	**hus**	he͞wss

---

* The **r** should not be pronounced when reading this transcription.

	2) when short, a little more like the **u** of put; a very difficult sound	ew	**full**	fewl
y	pronounce the **ee** of **bee** and then round your lips without moving your tongue; the sound can be long or short	e̅w̅ ew	**vy** **syster**	ve̅w̅ **sew**sterr
å	1) when long, like **aw** in **raw,** but with the tongue a little higher in the mouth	oa	**gå**	goa
	2) when short, like **o** in **hot**	o	**sång**	song
ä	1) when followed by **r,** like **a** in **man,** long or short	æ̅ æ	**ära** **värka**	æ̅rah værkah
	2) elsewhere, like **e** in **get**; long or short	ai eh	**läsa** **bäst**	**lais**sah behst
ö	like **ur** in **fur,** but with the lips rounded and without any r-sound; long or short; when followed by **r,** it is pronounced with the mouth a little more open	u̅r̅ ur	**röd** **köld** **öra**	ru̅r̅d khurld u̅r̅rah

Intonation

Swedish sometimes uses intonation (or more correctly "tones") to distinguish between words. Without considerable training, a foreigner can't recognize the tones, much less use them correctly. Because Swedes understand the difficulty, they don't expect foreigners to use intonation. Thus we haven't shown the tones in our transcriptions.

Notes

1. Throughout the pronunciation sections of this book you will notice that some letters are placed in parentheses [e.g. **mew**ker(t)]. In absolutely correct Swedish you should pronounce all the sounds indicated. However, in current usage most Swedes omit the sounds that are shown in parentheses. Take your pick.
2. In Swedish alphabetical listings, words beginning with Å, Ä and Ö come right at the end, after Z.

Some basic expressions

Yes.	**Ja.**	yaa
No.	**Nej.**	nay
Please.	**Var så god.**	vaar soa gōōd
Thank you.	**Tack.**	tahk
Thank you very much.	**Tack så mycket.**	tahk soa **mew**ker(t)
No, thank you.	**Nej tack.**	nay tahk

Greetings

Good morning.	**God morgon.**	goo **mor**ron
Good afternoon.	**God middag.**	goo **mid**dah(g)
Good evening.	**God afton.**	goo **ahf**ton
Good night.	**God natt.**	goo naht
Good-bye.	**Adjö.**	ahyūr
See you later.	**Vi ses.**	vee sāyss
This is Mr/Mrs/ Miss...	**Herr/Fru/Fröken...**	hehr/frēw/frūrkern
How do you do?	**Goddag.***	goddaag
I'm very pleased to meet you.	**Angenämt.**	ahnyernaimt
How are you?	**Hur mår ni?**	hēwr moar nee
Very well, thanks, and you?	**Bara bra tack, och ni?**	**baa**rah braa tahk ok nee
Pardon?	**Förlåt?**	furr**loat**
Excuse me. (May I get past?)	**Ursäkta.**	ēw**r**sehtah
I beg your pardon?	**Förlåt?**	furr**loat**

* Generally people say "Goddag" and shake hands when introduced. "Hej" is an informal expression you'll hear all the time, similar to the American "Hi!".

Questions

Where?	**Var?**	vaar
Where is...?	**Var är...?**	vaar ӕr
Where are...?	**Var finns...?**	vaar finss
How?	**Hur?**	hewr
How much?	**Hur mycket?**	hewr mewker(t)
How many?	**Hur många?**	hewr mongah
When?	**När?**	nӕr
What?	**Vad?**	vaa(d)
Why?	**Varför?**	vahrfurr
Who?	**Vem?**	vehm
Which?	**Vilken?**	vilkern
What do you call this in Swedish?	**Vad heter det här på svenska?**	vaa(d) hāyterr dāy(t) hӕr poa svehnskah
What do you call that in Swedish?	**Vad heter det där på svenska?**	vaa(d) hāyterr dāy(t) dӕr poa svehnskah
What do you call these in Swedish?	**Vad kallas de här på svenska?**	vaa(d) kahlass deh hӕr poa svehnskah
What do you call those in Swedish?	**Vad kallas de där på svenska?**	vaa(d) kahlass deh dӕr poa svehnskah
What does this mean?	**Vad betyder det här?**	vaa(d) bertewderr dāy(t) hӕr
What does that mean?	**Vad betyder det där?**	vaa(d) bertewderr dāy(t) dӕr

Do you speak...?

Do you speak English?	**Talar ni engelska?**	taalahr nee ehngerlskah
Is there anyone here who speaks...?	**Finns det någon här som talar...?**	finss dāy(t) noagon hӕr som taalahr

I don't speak (much) Swedish.	Jag talar inte (mycket) svenska.	yaa(g) taalahr inter (mewker[t]) svehnskah
Could you speak more slowly?	Kan ni tala lite långsammare, tack?	kahn nee taalah leeter longsahmahrer tahk
Could you repeat that?	Kan ni säga om det där, tack?	kahn nee sehyah om dāy(t) dær tahk
Please write it down.	Skulle ni kunna skriva det?	skewler nee kewnah skreevah dāy(t)
Can you translate (this) for me?	Kan ni översätta (det här) för mig?	kahn nee ūrver^rsehtah (dāy[t] hær) fūrr may
Please point to the phrase in the book.	Var snäll och peka på meningen i boken.	vaar snehl ok pāykah poa māyningern ee bōōkern
Just a minute. I'll see if I can find it in this book.	Ett ögonblick så skall jag se om jag hittar det i den här boken.	eht ūrgonblik soa skahl yaa(g) sāy om yaa(g) hittahr dāy(t) ee dehn hær bōōkern
I understand.	Jag förstår.	yaa(g) fur^rstoar
I don't understand.	Jag förstår inte.	yaa(g) fur^rstoar inter
Do you understand?	Förstår ni?	fur^rstoar nee

Can...

Can I have...?	Kunde jag få...?	kewnder yaa(g) foa
Can we have...?	Kunde vi få...?	kewnder vee foa
Can you show me...?	Kan ni visa mig...?	kahn nee veessah may
I can't.	Det kan jag inte.	dāy(t) kahn yaa(g) inter
Can you tell me?	Skulle ni kunna säga mig?	skewler nee kewnah sehyah may
Can you help me?	Skulle ni kunna hjälpa mig?	skewler nee kewnah yehlpah may
Can I help you?	Kan jag hjälpa er?	kahn yaa(g) yehlpah āyr
Can you direct me to...?	Skulle ni kunna visa mig vägen till...?	skewler nee kewnah veessah may vaigern til

Wanting…

It is too brusque in Swedish to say "I want". Use the more polite:

I'd like…	**Jag skulle vilja ha…**	yaa(g) **skew**ler **vil**yah haa
We'd like…	**Vi skulle vilja ha…**	vee **skew**ler **vil**yah haa
What do you want?	**Vad skulle ni vilja ha?**	vaa(d) **skew**ler nee **vil**yah haa
Give me…	**Kan ni ge mig…**	kahn nee yāȳ may
Give it to me.	**Kan ni ge mig det.**	kahn nee yāȳ may dāȳ(t)
Bring me…	**Kan ni ge mig…**	kahn nee yāȳ may
Bring it to me.	**Kan ni ge mig det?**	kahn nee yāȳ may dāȳ(t)
I'm looking for…	**Jag letar efter…**	yaa(g) **lāȳ**tahr **ehf**terr
Show me…	**Kan ni visa mig…**	kahn nee **vees**sah may
Show it to me.	**Kan ni visa mig det.**	kahn nee **vees**sah may dāȳ(t)
I'm hungry.	**Jag är hungrig.**	yaa(g) ǣr **hewng**ri(g)
I'm thirsty.	**Jag är törstig.**	yaa(g) ǣr tur^r**sti**(g)
I'm tired.	**Jag är trött.**	yaa(g) ǣr trurt
I'm lost.	**Jag hittar inte.**	yaa(g) **hit**tahr **in**ter
It's important.	**Det är viktigt.**	dāȳ(t) ǣr **vik**tit
It's urgent.	**Det är brådskande.**	dāȳ(t) ǣr **bro(d)**skahnder
Hurry up!	**Skynda på!**	**shewn**dah poa

It is/There is…

It is…	**Det är…**	dāȳ(t) ǣr
Is it…?	**Är det…**	ǣr dāȳ(t)
It isn't…	**Det är inte…**	dāȳ(t) ǣr **in**ter

There is/are...	Det finns...	dāy(t) finss
Is there/Are there...?	Finns det...?	finss dāy(t)
There isn't/aren't...	Det finns inte...	dāy(t) finss inter
There isn't any at all.	Det finns inte alls.	dāy(t) finss inter ahlss
There aren't any at all.	Det finns inga alls.	dāy(t) finss ingah ahlss

It's...

big/small	stor/liten	stoor/leetern
quick/slow	snabb/långsam	snahb/longsahm
early/late	tidig/sen	teedi(g)/sāyn
cheap/expensive	billig/dyr	billi(g)/dēwr
near/far	nära/avlägsen	nǣrah/aavlehgsern
hot/cold	varm/kall	vahrm/kahl
full/empty	full/tom	fewl/toom
easy/difficult	enkel/svår	ehnkerl/svoar
heavy/light	tung/lätt	tewng/leht
open/shut	öppen/stängd	urpern/stehngd
right/wrong	rätt/fel	reht/fāyl
old/new	gammal/ny	gahmahl/nēw
old/young	gammal/ung	gahmahl/ewng
next/last	nästa/sista	nehstah/sistah
beautiful/ugly	vacker/ful	vahkerr/fēwl
free (vacant)/occupied	ledig/upptagen	lāydi(g)/ewptaagern
good/bad	bra/dålig	braa/doali(g)
better/worse	bättre/sämre	behtrer/sehmrer
here/there	här/där	hǣr/dǣr
now/then	nu/då	nēw/doa

Quantities

a little/a lot	**lite/en mängd**	leeter/ehn mehngd
much/many	**mycket/många**	mewker(t)/mongah
more/less	**mera/mindre**	māyrah/mindrer
enough/too much	**tillräckligt/för mycket**	tilrehklit/fürr mewker(t)
some(any)/none	**några/inga**	noagrah/ingah

Prepositions

at	**vid**	veed
on	**på**	poa
in	**i**	ee
to	**till**	til
from	**från**	froan
inside	**inne**	inner
outside	**ute**	ēwter
up/upstairs	**uppe**	ewper
down/downstairs	**nere**	nāyrer
for	**för**	fürr
after	**efter**	ehfter
before (time)	**innan**	innahn
before (place)	**framför**	frahmfurr
with	**med**	māyd
without	**utan**	ēwtahn
through	**genom**	yāynom
toward(s)	**mot**	mōot
until	**till dess**	til dehss
during	**under det att**	ewnderr dāy(t) aht

...and a few more useful words

and	**och**	ok
or	**eller**	ehlerr
not	**inte**	inter
nothing	**ingenting**	ingernting
none	**inga**	ingah
very	**mycket**	mewker(t)
too(also)	**även(också)**	aivern (oksoa)
soon	**snart**	snaa't
perhaps	**kanske**	kahnsher

Arrival

You've arrived. Whether you've come by ship or plane, you'll have to go through passport and customs formalities. (For car/border control, see page 146.)

There's certain to be somebody around who speaks English. That's why we're making this a brief section. What you really want is to be off to your hotel in the shortest possible time. And here are the steps to get these formalities out of the way quickly.

Passport control

Here's my passport.	**Här är mitt pass.**	hær ær mit pahss
I'll be staying...	**Jag tänker stanna...**	yaa(g) **tehn**kerr **stah**nah
a few days	**några dagar**	**noa**grah **daa**(gah)r
a week	**en vecka**	ehn **vehk**ah
two weeks	**två veckor**	tvoa **vehk**oor
a month	**en månad**	ehn **moa**nahd
I don't know yet.	**Jag vet inte ännu.**	yaa(g) vāyt inter **ehn**ew
I'm here on holiday.	**Jag är här på semester.**	yaa(g) ær hær poa seh**mehs**terr
I'm here on business.	**Jag är här i affärer.**	yaa(g) ær hær ee ah**fær**err
I'm just passing through.	**Jag är bara på genomresa.**	yaa(g) ær **baa**rah poa **yāy**nomrāyssah

If the going gets tough:

I'm sorry, I don't understand.	**Ursäkta mig. Jag förstår inte.**	**ēw**r**sehk**tah may. yaa(g) furr**stoar** inter
Is there anyone here who speaks English?	**Finns det någon här som talar engelska?**	finss dāy(t) **noa**gon hær som **taa**lahr **ehng**erlskah

Customs

The chart below shows you what you can bring in duty free (the allowances in parentheses are for non-European residents).*

Cigarettes		Cigars		Tobacco grams	Spirits		Wine
200 (400)	or	50 (100)	or	250 (500)	1 (1)	and	1 (1)

At major airports, Sweden has adopted the modified honour system of customs controls. After collecting your luggage you have a choice. If you have nothing to declare, follow the green channel. You won't have to open your bags—unless there's a spot check. If you have items to declare leave by the doorway marked with a red arrow.

I have nothing to declare.	**Jag har ingenting att förtulla.**	yaa(g) haar ingernting aht fur**'tewlah**
I have a...	**Jag har en...**	yaa(g) haar ehn
carton of cigarettes bottle of whisky bottle of wine	**limpa cigarretter flaska whisky flaska vin**	**limp**ah siggah**rehterr flahsk**ah wiski **flahsk**ah veen
Must I pay on this?	**Måste jag betala för det här?**	**moster** yaa(g) ber**taal**ah fürr day(t) **hær**
It's for my personal use.	**Det är för mitt personliga bruk.**	day(t) **ær** fürr mit pæ**'soon**liggah brewk

* All allowances are subject to change.

Passet, tack.	Your passport, please.
Har ni någonting att förtulla?	Have you anything to declare?
Var vänlig och öppna det här.	Please open this.
Det här måste ni betala tull för.	You'll have to pay duty on this.
Har ni något mer bagage?	Have you any more luggage?

Baggage—Porters

In the absence of porters, you'll find do-it-yourself luggage trolleys at the airport. You might find porters at the railway stations, but they are becoming scarce.

Where are the luggage trolleys?	**Var finns bagage-kärrorna?**	vaar finss bah**gaash**-khǣrornah
Porter!	**Bärare!**	**bǣ**rahrer
That's mine.	**Det där är mitt.**	dāy(t) dǣr ǣr mit
That's my...	**Det är min...**	dāy(t) ǣr min
bag/suitcase	**väska/kappsäck**	**veh**skah/**kahp**sehk
That...one.	**Den...där.**	dehn...dǣr
big/small	**stora/lilla**	**stōō**rah/**lil**lah
blue/brown	**blå/bruna**	bloa/**brēw**nah
black/plaid	**svarta/rutiga**	**svah^r**tah/**rēw**ti(g)ah
There's one piece missing.	**Det fattas ett kolli.**	dāy(t) **faht**tahss eht **kol**li
Take these bags to the...	**Var vänlig och tag de här väskorna till...**	vaar **vehn**li(g) ok taa(g) deh hǣr **veh**skoo^rnah til
bus	**bussen**	**bews**sern
luggage lockers	**väskförvarings-facken**	**vehsk**furrvaarings-fahkern
taxi	**en taxi**	ehn **tah**ksi
How much is that?	**Hur mycket blir det?**	hēwr **mew**kert(t) bleer dāy(t)

Changing money

You'll find a bank at most arrival points. If it's closed, you can change money at your hotel. There'll be only a slight difference in the exchange rate. Full details on money and currency exchange: pages 134-136.

Where's the nearest currency exchange office?	**Var ligger närmaste växelkontor?**	vaar liggerr nærmahster vehkserlkontōōr
Can you change these traveller's cheques?	**Kan ni växla de här resecheckerna?**	kahn nee vehkslah deh hær raysserkhehke'nah
I want to change some...	**Jag skulle vilja växla några...**	yaa(g) skewler vilyah vehkslah noagrah
dollars	**dollar**	dollahr
pounds	**pund**	pewnd
Can you change this into Swedish crowns?	**Kan ni växla det här till svenska kronor?**	kahn nee vehkslah day(t) hær til svehnskah krōōnoor
What's the rate of exchange?	**Vad är växelkursen?**	vaa(d) ær vehkserlkew'sern

Directions

How do I get to...?	**Hur kommer jag till...?**	hewr kommerr yaa(g) til
Where's the bus into town?	**Varifrån går bussen till stan?**	vaarifroan goar bewssern til staan
Where can I get a taxi?	**Var kan jag få tag på en taxi?**	vaar kahn yaa(g) foa taag poa ehn tahksi
Where can I rent a car?	**Var kan jag hyra en bil?**	vaar kahn yaa(g) hewrah ehn beel

Hotel reservations

Obviously, it's safest to book in advance. But if you haven't had the chance, check in at the hotel reservation service or tourist information office which you'll find in many terminals. Somebody there will certainly speak English.

FOR NUMBERS, see page 175

Car rental

Again, it's best to make arrangements in advance whenever possible. There are car rental firms at most airports and terminals. You're very likely to find someone there who will speak English, but if nobody does, try one of the following:

I'd like a...	Jag skulle vilja ha en...	yaa(g) skewler vilyah haa ehn
car	bil	beel
small car	liten bil	leetern beel
large car	stor bil	stoor beel
sports car	sportbil	spo'tbeel
station-wagon	stationsvagn	stahshoonsvahngn
I'd like it for...	Jag skulle vilja ha den...	yaa(g) skewler vilyah haa dehn
a day/4 days	en dag/4 dagar	ehn daa(g)/4 daa(gah)r
a week/2 weeks	en vecka/2 veckor	ehn vehkah/2 vehkoor
What's the charge per...?	Vad kostar det per...?	vaa(d) kostahr day(t) pær
day/week	dag/vecka	daa(g)/vehkah
Does that include mileage?	Ingår kilometer-priset?	ingoar khillo-mmayterrpreessert
What's the charge per kilometre?	Vad är kilometer-priset?	vaa(d) ær khillo-mmayterrpreessert
Is petrol (gasoline) included?	Ingår bensinkost-naderna i priset?	inhoar behnsseenkost-nahderrnah ee preessert
I want full insurance.	Jag skulle vilja ha helförsäkring.	yaa(g) skewler vilyah haa haylfur'saikring
I'll be doing about ...kilometers.	Jag kommer att köra ungefär... kilometer.	yaa(g) kommerr aht khurrah ewnyer-fær...khillommayterr
What's the deposit?	Hur stor är handpenningen?	hewr stoor ær hahn(d)pehningern
I have a credit card.	Jag har kreditkort.	yaa(g) haar krehdeet-koo't
Here's my driving licence.	Här är mitt kör-kort.	hær ær mit khurrkoo't

FOR CAR, see page 142

| Is there a map of ...in the car? | **Finns det någon karta över...i bilen?** | finss dāy(t) noagon kaa`tah ūrverr...ee beelern |

Note: In Sweden you can drive for three months on your own licence. But check whether an international licence is required for other countries you may visit.

Taxis

All taxis have meters. After midnight an extra charge is added.

Where can I get a taxi?	**Var kan jag få tag på en taxi?**	vaar kahn yaa(g) foa taag poa ehn **tahksi**
Get me a taxi, please.	**Kan ni skaffa mig en taxi?**	kahn nee **skahfah** may ehn **tahksi**
How far is it to...?	**Hur långt är det till...?**	hēwr longt ær dāy(t) til
Please take me to...	**Kör mig till...tack.**	khūrr may til...tahk
this address	**den här adressen**	dehn hær ahdrehssern
the town centre	**centrum**	sehntrewm
the...Hotel	**hotell...**	hotehl
Turn...at the next corner.	**Kör till...vid nästa gathörn.**	khūrr til...veed nehstah gaathūr`n
left/right	**vänster/höger**	**vehnsterr/hūrgerr**
Go straight ahead.	**Kör rakt fram.**	khūrr raakt frahm
Stop here, please.	**Stanna här, tack.**	stahnah hær tahk
I'm in a hurry.	**Jag har bråttom.**	yaa(g) haar **brottom**
Could you drive more slowly?	**Kan ni köra lite långsammare, tack?**	kahn nee **khūrrah** leeter longsahmahrer tahk
Could you help me to carry my bags?	**Skulle ni kunna hjälpa mig att bära mina väskor?**	skewler nee kewnah yehlpah may aht bærah meenah vehskoor

FOR TIPPING, see inside back-cover

Hotel—Other accommodation

In major tourist centres it's essential to book in advance
—and to have your reservation confirmed—during the
height of the season. If you're stranded, most towns have
a tourist information office.

There is no official classification system for hotels in
Sweden. In the major towns top-class hotels up to international standards are to be found. Throughout the
country, accommodation as described below is plentiful.

Note that breakfast is not normally included in the room
price.

Familjehotell (fahmilyerhotehl)	In summer a number of hotels, particularly in the major cities, offer special rates for families with children in rooms with three to six beds.
Turisthotell (tewristhotehl)	Small and simple but clean and comfortable, many tourist hotels and boarding-houses are found in summer resorts and winter sports centres. As a rule, breakfast and dinner are included. Rates are usually based on a three-day stay.
Sommarhotell (sommahrhotehl)	In Stockholm, Gothenburg and Lund, modern blocks of student flats are converted for tourists in the summer. These hotels are particularly suitable for group accommodation.
Motell (mootehl)	Accommodation for motorists, usually with restaurant and car-service facilities. All modern with high standards.
Privatrum (privvaatrewm)	Local and regional tourist associations can recommend rooms in private homes.
Stugor (stewgoor)	Summer chalets, rather expensive, are let by the week. Start looking well in advance—ask the local tourist office for information.
Vandrarhem (vahndrahrhehm)	The Swedish Touring Club (STF) operates these comfortable, cheap hostels all over Sweden.

You'll have no language problems in luxury and first-class hotels where there's always someone who speaks English. Here we are concerned rather with the smaller and middle-grade hotels and boarding-houses where the staff may speak nothing but Swedish.

Checking in—Reception

My name is...	**Mitt namn är...**	mit nahmn __är__
I have a reservation.	**Jag har beställt rum.**	yaa(g) haar ber**stehlt** rewm
I wrote to you last month.	**Jag skrev till er i förra månaden.**	yaa(g) skra͞yv til a͞yr ee furrah **moa**nahdern
Here is the confirmation.	**Här är bekräftelsen.**	hǟr ǟr ber**krehf**terlsern
The tourist office sent us here.	**Turistbyrån skickade oss hit.**	tewrist**be͞w**roan **shik**kahder oss heet
They telephoned from the airport/railway-station.	**De ringde från flygplatsen/ järnvägsstationen.**	deh **ring**der froan **fle͞wg**plahtsern/yǟ**r**n- vaigsstahsho͞onern
No, I haven't a reservation.	**Nej, jag har inte beställt.**	nay yaa(g) haar **in**ter ber**stehlt**
I'd like...	**Jag skulle vilja ha...**	yaa(g) **skew**ler **vil**yah haa
a single/double room	**ett enkelrum/ dubbelrum**	eht **ehn**kerlrewm/ **dew**berlrewm
two single rooms	**två enkelrum**	tvoa **ehn**kerlrewm
a room with a bath/ shower	**ett rum med bad/ dusch**	eht rewm ma͞yd baad/ dewsh
a room with a balcony	**ett rum med balkong**	eht rewm ma͞yd **bahl**kong
a room with a view	**ett rum med utsikt**	eht rewm ma͞yd **e͞wt**sikt
a suite	**en svit**	ehn sveet
We'd like a room...	**Vi skulle vilja ha ett rum...**	vee **skew**ler **vil**yah haa eht rewm
in the front	**på framsidan**	poa **frahm**seedahn
at the back	**på baksidan**	poa **baak**seedahn
facing the sea	**mot havet**	mo͞ot **haa**vert
facing the courtyard	**mot gården**	mo͞ot **goa**rdern

It must be quiet.	Det måste vara lugnt.	dāy(t) moster vaarah lewngt
Can you provide a cot/an extra bed?	Kan ni ordna en barnsäng/en extra säng?	kahn nee o^rdnah ehn baa^rnsehng/ehn ehkstrah sehng
Is there…?	Finns det…?	finss dāy(t)
heating	värme	væermer
a radio/television in the room	radio/TV på rummet	raadio/tāyveh poa rewmert
a laundry service	tvättinrättning	tvehtinrehtning
room service	rumsbetjäning	rewmsberkhaining
hot water	varmvatten	vahrmvahtern
running water	rinnande vatten	rinnahnder vahtern
a private toilet	en egen toalett	ehn āygern tooahleht
What floor is it on?	Vilken våning ligger det på?	vilkern voaning liggerr dāy(t) poa
Is there a lift (elevator)?	Finns det hiss?	finss dāy(t) hiss
Is there a sauna/ swimming-pool?	Finns det bastu/ simbassäng?	finss dāy(t) bahstew/ simbahssehng

How much?

What's the price…?	Vad kostar det…?	vaa(d) kostahr dāy(t)
per week	per vecka	pær vehkah
per night	per natt	pær naht
for bed and breakfast	ett rum med frukost	eht rewm māyd frewkost
excluding meals	utan måltider	ewtahn moalteederr
for half board	halvpension	hahlvpehnshōōn
for full board	helpension	hāylpehnshōōn
Does that include…?	Ingår…?	ingoar
breakfast	frukost	frewkost
meals	måltiderna	moalteeder^rnah
service	dricks	driks
Is there any reduction for children?	Ger ni rabatt för barn?	yāyr nee rahbaht furr baa^rn
Do you charge for the baby?	Tar ni betalt för spädbarn?	taar nee bertaalt furr spai(d)baa^rn
Haven't you anything cheaper?	Har ni ingenting billigare?	haar nee ingernting billiggahrer

FOR NUMBERS, see page 175

How long?

We'll be staying...	Vi tänker stanna...	vee **tehn**kerr **stah**nah
overnight only	bara över natten	**baa**rah **ūr**verr **nah**tern
a few days	några dagar	**noa**grah **daa**(gah)r
a week (at least)	en vecka (minst)	ehn **vehk**ah (minsst)
I don't know yet.	Jag vet inte ännu.	yaa(g) vāyt **int**er **eh**new

Decision

May I see the room?	Kan jag få se på rummet?	kahn yaa(g) foa sāy poa **rew**mert
No, I don't like it.	Nej, jag tycker inte om det.	nay yaa(g) **tewk**err **int**er om dāy(t)
It's too...	Det är för...	dāy(t) ær fūrr
cold/hot	kallt/varmt	kahlt/**vahr**mt
dark/small	mörkt/litet	**murr**kt/**lee**tert
noisy	bullrigt	**bewl**rit
I asked for a room with a bath.	Jag bad om ett rum med bad.	yaa(g) baa(d) om eht rewm māyd baad
Do you have anything...?	Har ni någonting...?	haar nee **noa**gonting
better/bigger	bättre/större	**beht**rer/**stur**rer
cheaper/quieter	billigare/lugnare	**bil**liggahrer/ **lewng**nahrer
higher up	högre upp	**hūr**grer ewp
lower down	lägre ner	**laig**rer nāyr
Do you have a room with a better view?	Har ni ett rum med bättre utsikt?	haar nee eht rewm māyd **beht**rer **ēwt**sikt
That's fine. I'll take it.	Det är bra. Jag tar det.	dāy(t) ær braa. yaa(g) taar dāy(t)

The bill (check)

Bills are usually paid weekly or upon departure if you stay less than a week. Some hotels offer a reduction of 50 per cent for children under 12, if sleeping on an extra bed in the same room.

FOR DAYS OF THE WEEK, see page 181

Tipping

It is not necessary to tip the chambermaid or other members of the staff, unless they perform special services. But do tip the porter when he carries the luggage to your room.

Registration

Upon arrival at a hotel or boarding house you'll be asked to fill in a registration form *(inskrivningsblankett)*. It asks your name, home address, passport number and further destination. It's almost certain to carry an English translation. If it doesn't, ask the desk-clerk *(portiern— po⌐tkhāy⌐n)*:

What does this mean?	**Vad betyder det här?**	vaa(d) ber**tēw**derr dāy(t) hær

The desk-clerk will probably ask for your passport and may want to ask you the following questions:

Kan jag få se ert pass?	May I see your passport?
Vill ni vara vänlig och fylla i den här blanketten?	Would you mind filling in this registration form?
Var vänlig och skriv under här.	Please sign here.
Hur länge tänker ni stanna?	How long will you be staying?

What's my room number?	**Vad är rumsnumret?**	vaa(d) ær **rewms**newmrert
Will you have our bags sent up?	**Kan ni sända upp bagaget, tack?**	kahn nee **sehn**dah ewp bah**gaas**hert tahk

FOR TIPPING, see also inside back-cover

Service, please

bellboy	**pickolon**	pikkolon
maid	**städerskan**	staider'skahn
manager	**direktören**	dirrerktūrrern
room service	**rumsbetjäningen**	rewmsberkhainingern
switchboard operator	**telefonisten**	tehlerfonnistern
waiter	**kyparen**	kh$\overline{ew}$pahrern
waitress	**servitrisen**	sehrvitreessern

Call the waiter *hovmästaren* (**hoav**mehstahrern) which is in fact the word for headwaiter. The waitress should be addressed as *fröken* (**frū**rkern).

General requirements

Please ask the maid to come up.	**Var vänlig och be städerskan komma upp.**	vaar **vehn**li(g) ok b$\overline{ay}$ staider'skahn kommah ewp
Who is it?	**Vem är det?**	vehm ær d$\overline{ay}$(t)
Come in!	**Kom in!**	kom in
Is there a bath on this floor?	**Finns det badrum på den här våningen?**	finss d$\overline{ay}$(t) baadrewm poa dehn hær voaningern
How does this shower work?	**Hur fungerar duschen?**	h$\overline{ew}$r fewng$\overline{ay}$rahr dewshern
Where's the plug for the razor?	**Var är kontakten för rakapparaten?**	vaar ær kon**tahk**tern fürr **raa**kahpahraatern
What's the voltage here?	**Vad är strömstyrkan?**	vaa(d) ær strurmstewrkahn
Can we have breakfast in our room?	**Kan vi få frukost på rummet?**	kahn vee foa **frew**kost poa **rew**mert
I'd like to leave these in your safe.	**Jag skulle vilja lämna det här i kassaskåpet.**	yaa(g) **skew**ler vilyah **lehm**nah d$\overline{ay}$(t) hær ee kahssahskoapert
Can you find me a baby-sitter?	**Skulle ni kunna ordna barnvakt?**	**skew**ler nee **kew**nah oa'dnah **baa**'nvahkt

May I have a/an some...?	Kan jag få...?	kahn yaa(g) foa
ashtray	en askkopp	ehn ahskop
bath-towel	ett badlakan	eht baadlaakahn
extra blanket	en extra filt	ehn ehkstrah filt
envelopes	några kuvert	noagrah kewvær
(more) hangers	(fler) klädhängare	(flehr) klai(d)-hehngahrer
ice cubes	några isbitar	noagrah eessbeetahr
extra pillow	en extra kudde	ehn ehkstrah kewder
reading-lamp	en läslampa	ehn laislahmpah
soap	en tvål	ehn tvoal
writing-paper	lite brevpapper	leeter brayvpahperr
Where's the...?	Var är...?	vaar ær
barber's	frisörsalongen	frissurrsahlongern
bathroom	badrummet	baadrewmert
beauty salon	skönhetssalongen	shurnhaytssahlongern
dining-room	matsalen	maatsaalern
hairdresser's	damfriseringen	daamfrissayringern
restaurant	restaurangen	rehstorrahngern
television room	TV-rummet	tayveh-rewmert
toilet	toaletten	tooahlehtern

Breakfast

The Swedish breakfast consists of coffee or tea and bread with butter and cheese, jam or marmalade. Many people also have ham and eggs or yoghurt, and most hotels are now used to providing a breakfast of the British or American type.

I'll have a/an/ some...	Jag skall be att få...	yaa(g) skahl bay aht foa
bacon and eggs	bacon och ägg	baykon ok ehg
cereals (hot)	gröt	grurt
cornflakes	flingor	flingoor
eggs	ägg	ehg
boiled egg	kokt ägg	kookt ehg
soft/medium/ hard	löskokt/lagom/ hårdkokt	lurskookt/laagom/ hoar'dkookt
fried eggs	stekta ägg	stayktah ehg
poached eggs	förlorade ägg	fur'loorahder ehg
scrambled eggs	äggröra	ehgrurrah

fruit juice	fruktjuice	frewktyōoss
grapefruit	grapefrukt	graypfrewkt
orange	apelsin	ahperlsseen
pineapple/tomato	ananas/tomat	ahnahnahss/tommaat
ham and eggs	skinka och ägg	shinkah ok ehg
jam	sylt	sewlt
marmalade	marmelad	mahrmerlaad
omelet	omelett	om(er)leht
pancakes	pannkakor	pahnkaakoor
porridge	gröt	grurt
sausages	korv	korv
sour(ed) milk	filmjölk	feelmyurlk
toast	rostat bröd	rostaht brurd
May I have some...?	Kan jag få lite...?	kahn yaa(g) foa leeter
hot/cold milk	varm/kall mjölk	vahrm/kahl myurlk
cream/sugar	grädde/socker	grehder/sokkerr
bread/rolls	bröd/småfranska	brurd/smoafrahnskah
butter	smör	smurr
salt/pepper	salt/peppar	sahlt/pehpahr
coffee/tea	kaffe/te	kahfer/tay
hot chocolate	varm choklad	vahrm shoklaa(d)
lemon/honey	citron/honung	sitrōōn/hoanewng
hot water	varmt vatten	vahrmt vahtern
Could you bring me a...?	Skulle jag kunna få...?	skewler yaa(g) kewnah foa
plate	en tallrik	ehn tahlrik
glass/cup	ett glas/en kopp	eht glaass/ehn kop
knife/fork	en kniv/en gaffel	ehn kneev/ehn gahferl
napkin (serviette)	en servett	ehn særveht
spoon	en sked	ehn shayd

Difficulties

The...doesn't work.	...fungerar inte.	fewngayrahr inter
air-conditioner	luftkonditio-neringen	lewftkondishon-nayringern
fan	fläkten	flehktern
heating	värmen	værmern
light	ljuset	yewssert
radio	radion	raadion
tap	kranen	kraanern
toilet	toaletten	tooahlehtern

FOR EATING OUT, see pages 38-64

HOTEL SERVICE

The wash-basin is clogged.	Det är stopp i handfatet.	day(t) ær stop ee hahn(d)faatert
The window is jammed.	Fönstret går inte att få upp.	furnstrert goar inter aht foa ewp
The blind is stuck.	Rullgardinen har hakat upp sig.	rewlgah^rdeenern haar haakaht ewp say
I can't open the wardrobe.	Jag kan inte öppna garderobsdörren.	yaa(g) kahn inter urpnah gah^rderroabsdurrern
The door won't lock.	Det går inte att låsa dörren.	day(t) goar inter aht loassah durrern
These aren't my shoes.	Detta är inte mina skor.	dehtah ær inter meenah skoor
This isn't my laundry.	Det här är inte min tvätt.	day(t) hær ær inter min tveht
There's no hot water.	Det finns inget varmvatten.	day(t) finss ingert vahrmvahtern
I've left my key in my room.	Jag har glömt nyckeln på rummet.	yaa(g) haar glurmt newkeln poa rewmert
The...is broken.	...är sönder.	ær surnderr
lamp	lampan	lahmpahn
plug	stickkontakten	stikkontahktern
switch	strömbrytaren	strurmbrewtahrern
Can you get it repaired?	Kan ni laga den?	kahn nee laagah dehn

Telephone—Mail—Callers

Can you get me...	Kan ni ge mig..., tack?	kahn nee yay may... tahk
Did anyone telephone me?	Har någon ringt mig?	haar noagon ringt may
Do you have any stamps?	Har ni några frimärken?	haar nee noagrah freemærkern
Would you please mail this for me?	Skulle ni kunna skicka det här för mig?	skewler nee kewnah shikkah day(t) hær furr may
Are there any messages for me?	Finns det några meddelanden till mig?	finss day(t) noagrah mayderlahndern til may

FOR POST OFFICE and TELEPHONE, see pages 137-141

Checking out

May I please have my bill?	Jag skall be att få räkningen.	yaa(g) skahl bay aht foa raikningern
I'm leaving early tomorrow. Please have my bill ready.	Jag reser tidigt i morgon bitti. Var vänlig och ha räkningen klar.	yaa(g) raysserr teedit ee morron bitti. vaar vehnli(g) ok haa raikningern klaar
We'll be checking out soon/around noon.	Vi lämnar snart/ vid tolv-tiden.	vee lehmnahr snaa^rt/ veed tolv-teedern
When is check-out time?	Hur dags måste man lämna rummet?	hewr dahgss moster mahn lehmnah rewmmert
I must leave at once.	Jag måste fara genast.	yaa(g) moster faarah yaynahst
Is everything included?	Är allt inräknat?	ær ahlt inraiknaht
You've made a mistake in this bill, I think.	Jag tror ni har gjort ett fel på räkningen.	yaa(g) troor nee haar yoo^rt eht fayl poa raikningern
Can you get us a taxi?	Kan ni skaffa oss en taxi?	kahn nee skahffah oss ehn tahksi
When's the next... to...?	När går nästa... till...?	nær goar nehstah... til
bus/train/plane	buss/tåg/flygplan	bewss/toag/flewgplaan
Would you send someone to bring down our baggage?	Kan vi få ner bagaget?	kahn vee foa nayr bahgaashert
We're in a great hurry.	Vi har mycket bråttom.	vee haar mewker(t) brottom
Here's the forwarding address.	Här är eftersänd-ningsadressen.	hær ær ehfterr-sehndningsahdrehssern
You have my home address.	Ni har min bostadsadress.	nee haar min boostaads-ahdrehss
It's been a very enjoyable stay.	Det har varit en mycket trevlig vistelse.	day(t) haar vaarit ehn mewker(t) trayvli(g) visterlser
I hope we'll come again sometime.	Jag hoppas vi snart kan komma tillbaka.	yaa(g) hoppahss vee snaa^rt kahn kommah tilbaakah

FOR TAXI, see page 27

HOTEL SERVICE

Eating out

Eating places in Sweden range from the chic to the quick. The following rundown will help you know what to look for to suit your mood.

Restaurang
(rehstorrahng)

Restaurants range from the plain and simple to the luxury class but without any official rating system.

In luxury restaurants you often get French-inspired food, although you will also find excellent Swedish specialities. Usually the décor is extravagant—and so is the bill! On weekends you must book a table in advance.

First-class restaurants serve fine food but in a more rustic atmosphere, often in transformed medieval cellars, located in the old part of the town. To ensure a table, reserve in advance.

There is a rapid growth of small restaurants, not too expensive and in a rustic or intimate atmosphere. The food is generally good. Wine or beer may be served, but nothing stronger.

Fiskrestaurång
(fiskrehstorrahng)

Fish and seafood specialities.

Värdshus
(vae^rdshewss)

Old coaching inns, on the outskirts of town or in open country, with romantic décor and high standards of cooking.

Grillbar
(grilbaar)

Self-service hamburgers, steaks, chips, etc., usually with beer or non-alcoholic drinks only. Varied quality, possibly crowded.

Gatukök (**gaa**tewkhūrk)	Typically Scandinavian "kitchen on the street" for a quick bite before or after the cinema. Sausages or hamburgers with mashed potatoes or chips (french-fries), ice-cream and soft drinks.
Korvstånd (**korv**stond)	Swedish hot-dog stand. No drinks or ice-cream or frills.
Konditori (kondit**torree**)	A coffee shop for soft drinks, coffee and tea, ice-cream and pastry.
Cocktail bar ("cocktail bar")	Only in the bigger towns and hotels. Sometimes snacks are served along with the drinks.

The service charge is always included in the bill. Any tip above this is up to you.

Meal times

In this section we are primarily concerned with lunch and dinner. We assume you have already had breakfast at your hotel or boarding-house.

Lunch—the Swedes use the same word but pronounce it lewnsh—is normally served from 11.30 a.m. and dinner from 6 p.m. The word for dinner is *middag* [**mi**ddah(g)].

Meal times are more flexible than in some other European countries, and you'll find many restaurants will serve a meal at any hour of the afternoon.

Note that alcoholic beverages are not served before noon anywhere in Sweden.

FOR BREAKFAST, see page 34

Hungry?

If you're staying at a smaller hotel which doesn't have its own restaurant your first concern will probably be to find a good one to suit your pocket without the sometimes hazardous business of choosing one at random. So:

Are there any good, cheap restaurants around here?	**Finns det någon bra och billig restaurang i närheten?**	finss day(t) noagon braa ok billi(g) rehstorrahng ee nærhaytern
Can you recommend a good restaurant?	**Kan ni föreslå en bra restaurang?**	kahn nee furrersloa ehn braa rehstorrahng

If you want to be sure of getting a table in a well-known restaurant, it may be better to telephone in advance. Some of them close one day a week.

I would like to reserve a table for 3.	**Jag skulle vilja beställa ett bord för 3.**	yaa(g) skewler vilyah berstehlah eht boo'd furr 3
We will come at 1 o'clock.	**Vi kommer klockan 1.**	vee kommerr klokkahn 1

Asking and ordering

Good afternoon/ evening. I would like a table for 4.	**Goddag/god afton. Jag skulle vilja ha ett bord för 4.**	goddaag/goo ahfton. yaa(g) skewler vilyah haa eht boo'd furr 4
Could I have...?	**Skulle jag kunna få...?**	skewler yaa(g) kewnah foa
a table in the corner	**ett hörnbord**	eht hur'nboo'd
a table by the window	**ett fönsterbord**	eht furnsterrboo'd
a table outside	**ett bord ute**	eht boo'd ewter
a table on the terrace	**ett bord på terrassen**	eht boo'd poa tehrahssern
a quiet table somewhere	**ett lugnt bord någonstans**	eht lewngt boo'd noagonstahnss
Where are the toilets?	**Var ligger toaletten?**	vaar liggerr tooahlehtern

What time do you start serving lunch/dinner?	**Hur dags börjar ni servera lunch/middag?**	hewr dahgss **burr**yahr nee sær**vay**rah lewnsh/**middah**(g)
May I please have the menu/wine list?	**Kan jag få se matsedeln/vinlistan, tack?**	kahn yaa(g) foa say **maats**ayderln/**veen**listahn tahk
What's this?	**Vad är det här?**	vaa(d) ær day(t) hær
What do you recommend?	**Vad föreslår ni?**	vaa(d) **fur**rersloar nee

Vad önskar ni?	What would you like?
Jag rekommenderar det här.	I recommend this.
Vad önskar ni dricka?	What would you like to drink?
Vi har inte...	We haven't got...
Önskar ni...?	Do you want...?

Do you have...?	**Har ni...?**	haar nee
a set menu	**en dagens rätt**	ehn **daa**gerns reht
local dishes	**specialiteter från trakten**	spehssiahlit**ay**terr froan **trahk**tern
a children's menu	**en barnmatsedel**	ehn baa**r**nmaats**ay**derl
I'd like...	**Jag skulle vilja ha...**	yaa(g) **skew**ler **vil**yah haa
Is service included?	**Är dricksen inräknad?**	ær **drik**sern **in**raiknahd
Could we have a/an/some..., please?	**Kan vi få...tack?**	kahn vee foa...tahk
ashtray	**en askkopp**	ehn **ahs**kop
another chair	**en stol till**	ehn st**oo**l til
fingerbowl	**en sköljkopp**	ehn **shurl**ykop
fork	**en gaffel**	ehn **gah**fehl
glass	**ett glas**	eht glaass
knife	**en kniv**	ehn kneev
napkin	**en servett**	ehn sær**veht**
pepper-mill	**en pepparkvarn**	ehn **pehp**ahrkvaa**r**n
plate	**en tallrik**	ehn **tahl**rik

FOR COMPLAINTS, see page 59

EATING OUT

salt	lite salt	leeter sahlt
serviette	en servett	ehn sœrveht
spoon	en sked	ehn shāyd
toothpicks	några tandpetare	noagrah tahn(d)-pāytahrer
I'd like a/an/some...	Jag skulle vilja ha...	yaa(g) skewler vilyah haa
aperitif	en drink	ehn drink
appetizer	en förrätt	ehn fūrreht
beer	en öl	ehn ūrl
bread	lite bröd	leeter brūrd
butter	lite smör	leeter smūrr
cheese	lite ost	leeter oost
chips	pommes frites	pom frit
coffee	kaffe	kahfer
dessert	en efterrätt	ehn ehftreht
fish	fisk	fisk
french-fries	pommes frites	pom frit
fruit	frukt	frewkt
game	vilt	vilt
ice-cream	glass	glahss
lemon	citron	sitrōōn
lettuce	sallad	sahlahd
meat	kött	khurt
milk	mjölk	myurlk
mineral water	mineralvatten	minnerraalvahtern
mustard	lite senap	leeter sāynahp
noodles	nudlar	nēwdlahr
olive oil	olivolja	ooleevolyah
pepper	peppar	pehpahr
potatoes	potatis	potaatiss
poultry	kyckling	khewkling
rice	ris	reess
rolls	småfranska	smoafrahnskah
salt	salt	sahlt
sandwich	en smörgås	ehn smurrgoass
seafood	en skaldjursrätt	ehn skaalyēwʳsreht
seasoning	lite kryddor	leeter krewdoor
soup	soppa	soppah
starter	en förrätt	ehn fūrreht
sugar	socker	sokkerr
tea	te	tāy
vegetables	grönsaker	grūrnsaakerr
vinegar	vinäger	vinnaigerr
(iced) water	(is)vatten	(eess)vahtern
wine	vin	veen

What's on the menu?

Our menu is presented according to courses. Under the headings below you'll find alphabetical lists of dishes that might be offered on a Swedish menu with their English equivalents. You can also show the book to the waiter. If you want some fruit, for instance, show him the appropriate list and let him point to what's available. Use pages 41 and 42 for ordering in general.

Here then is our guide to good eating and drinking. Turn to the section you want.

Obviously, you aren't going to go through every course. If you've had enough say:

Nothing more, thanks.	**Ingenting mer, tack.**	ingernting māyr tahk

A word of warning before you sit down to your meal: "If you drink don't drive; if you drive don't drink!" The Swedish police are extremely severe on this point. A single glass of wine or beer is enough for you to lose your driving licence, and with larger amounts of alcohol the penalty runs to fines and automatic jail sentences. If you intend to consume any alcohol do as the Swedes do: walk, take a taxi or make sure that your driver does not touch a drop!

EATING OUT

Appetizers

Contrary to popular opinion, the Swedes don't spend all their time eating *smörgåsbord*. Nor is it usual to have both a smörgåsbord and a main course. A full-scale smörgåsbord is both filling and expensive. Many larger restaurants usually serve smörgåsbord at Sunday lunch (see page 46).

It's by no means the universal custom to take an appetizer before your main course. The Swedes themselves are usually content with a single dish, though for a special occasion one or other of the appetizers listed below will admirably enhance your meal.

We have divided this section into two parts. We start with the various standard appetizers, and tackle the smörgåsbord separately.

Appetizers can be grouped into five basic categories:

kallskuret
(kahlskewrert)
cold cuts, sausages, cured ham, etc.

sallader
(sahlahderr)
salads of fish, shellfish, meat, vegetables

sillbricka
(silbrikkah)
all manner of herring dishes — cured and marinated. Best accompanied by a glass or two of "snaps" and beer (see page 60)

småvarmt
(smoavahrmt)
small portions of fish, meat, vegetables or stews, served hot

smörgåsar
(smurrgoassahr)
open-faced sandwiches, buttered, topped with shrimps, smoked salmon, eggs and anchovies, herring, ham, liver paste or cheese

I'd like an appetizer.	Jag skulle vilja ha en förrätt.	yaa(g) skewler vilyah haa ehn fūrreht
What do you recommend?	Vad föreslår ni?	vaa(d) fūrrersloar nee

ansjovis	ahnshōōviss	anchovies, marinated sprats
blandade aptitretare	blahndahder ahpteet-rāytahrer	assorted appetizers
blåmusslor	bloamewssloor	mussels
böckling	burkling	smoked Baltic herring
gåslever	goasslāyverr	goose liver
hummer	hewmerr	lobster
juice	yōōss	fruit juice
ananas/apelsin/ grapefrukt/ tomat	ahnahnahss/ahperl-sseen/graypfrewkt/ tommaat	pineapple/orange/ grapefruit/tomato
kaviar	kahviahr	caviar
röd/svart	rūrd/svah°t	red/black
korv	korv	sausage
kokt/rökt	kookt/rūrkt	boiled/smoked
krabba	krahbah	crabmeat
kräftor	krehftoor	freshwater crayfish
lax	lahks	salmon
gravad/rökt	graavahd/rūrkt	cured/smoked
leverpastej	lāyverrpahstay	liver paste
löjrom	luryrom	bleak roe
matjesill med dill och lök	mahtyerssil māyd dil ok lūrk	herring with dill and onions
matjesill med gräddfil och gräslök	mahtyerssil māyd grehdfeel ok graislūrk	herring with sour cream and chives
oliver (fyllda)	ooleeverr (fewldah)	olives (stuffed)
omelett	om(er)leht	omelet
ost	oost	cheese
ostron	oostron	oysters
pastej	pahstay	pâté
rom	rom	roe
råbiff	roabif	beef tartar
rädisor	rehdissoor	radishes
sallad	sahlahd	salad
sardiner	sahrdeenerr	sardines
sikrom	seekrom	whitefish roe
sill	sil	herring
inlagd	inlahgd	marinated, pickled
i senapssås	ee sāynahpssoass	with mustard sauce

silltallrik	siltahlrik	assorted herring
skinka	shinkah	ham
kokt/rökt	kookt/rūrkt	boiled/smoked
smårätter	smoarehterr	fancy dishes
sparris	spahriss	asparagus
svamp	svahmp	mushrooms
ål	oal	eel
inkokt/rökt	inkookt/rūrkt	jellied/smoked
ägg och ansjovis	ehg ok ahnshōōviss	eggs and anchovies

Smörgåsbord

The Swedish *smörgåsbord* (**smurr**goasbōōᵣd), of ancient
origin, is well known abroad. In olden days this enor-
mous buffet was a common sight in homes and restaurants, especially around Christmas. Now the domestic
variety has been whittled down. But during Christmas
and in big hotels on Sundays and in summer you can
find these beautifully decorated tables brimming with
cold and warm delights. You start at one end of the
table, with herring, seafood, salads and other appetizers,
and return as many times as you want. The price is the
same for the big or small eater. During the Christmas
season the smörgåsbord is even bigger, but mostly based
on herring and pork (the same basic—food of the
Vikings).

Aquavit and beer go especially well with all this. It is
rare to drink wine with smörgåsbord. Normally this is
a lunchtime experience; it can take three hours.

Soups

| I'd like some soup. | **Jag skulle vilja ha soppa.** | yaa(g) skewler vilyah haa soppah |
| What do you recommend? | **Vad föreslår ni?** | vaa(d) fūrrersloar nee |

champinjonsoppa (shahmpinyoonsoppah)	mushroom soup
fisksoppa (fisksoppah)	fish soup
kålsoppa (koalsoppah)	cabbage soup
skaldjurssoppa (skaalyewrssoppah)	seafood soup
sparrissoppa (spahrissoppah)	asparagus soup
svartsoppa (svahrtsoppah)	black soup made from goose blood and giblets; speciality during the month of November
ärtsoppa (ærtsoppah)	yellow pea soup with smoked and salted pork; traditionally served Thursdays in winter as main course, along with hot sugared Swedish punch, and with pancakes as dessert

Salads

What salads do you have?	**Vilka sallader har ni?**	vilkah sahlahderr haar nee
grönsallad (grurnsahlahd)		lettuce, cucumber, tomatoes, parsley, dill, with oil and vinegar dressing; accompanies the main course
potatissallad (potaatissahlahd)		potato salad with chives and capers; served with sausages or other meat
räkcocktail (raikkoktayl)		fresh shrimp salad (served as an appetizer)
rödbetssallad (rurbaytssahlahd)		beetroot salad mixed with sour cream and mayonnaise, chives and onions
sillsallad (silsahlahd)		herring salad with potatoes, apples, beetroot and chives (appetizer)
vintersallad (vinterrsahlahd)		"winter salad" of grated carrots, apples and cabbage
västkustsallad (vehstkewstsahlahd)		Swedish speciality served as an appetizer with toast and butter: assorted seafood salad with mushrooms, tomatoes, green salad, cucumber, asparagus and dill

EATING OUT

Eggs

omelett	om(er)**leht**	omelet
med ost	māyd oost	with cheese
med skinka	māyd **shin**kah	with ham
med svamp	māyd svahmp	with mushrooms
med tomater	māyd tom**maa**terr	with tomatoes
kokt ägg	kookt ehg	boiled egg
löskokt	**lūrs**kookt	soft
lagom	**laa**gom	medium
hårdkokt	**hoa**ʳdkookt	hard
förlorat ägg	furˡ**loo**raht ehg	poached egg
stekt ägg	st**āy**kt ehg	fried egg
ägg och bacon	ehg ok **bay**kon	bacon and eggs
äggröra	ehg**rū**rrah	scrambled eggs

Fish and seafood

I'd like some fish.	**Jag skulle vilja ha fisk.**	yaa(g) **skew**ler **vil**yah haa fisk
What kind of seafood do you have?	**Vad har ni för skaldjur?**	vaa(d) haar nee fürr **skaal**y<u>ew</u>r
abborre	**ah**borrer	perch
böckling	**burk**ling	smoked Baltic herring
fiskbullar	**fisk**bewlahr	fishballs
flundra	**flęwn**drah	flatfish
forell	for**rehl**	trout
gädda	**yeh**dah	pike
havskräftor	**hahvs**krehftoor	crayfish (sea)
helgeflundra	**hel**yerflewndrah	halibut
hummer	**hew**merr	lobster
insjökräftor	**insh**ūrkrehftoor	crayfish (lake)
krabba	**krah**bah	crab
lake	**laa**ker	burbot
lax	lahks	salmon
laxöring	**lahks**ūrring	salmon trout
makrill	**mah**kril	mackerel
piggvar	**pig**vaar	turbot
rödspätta	**rūrs**pehtah	plaice
torsk	toʳsk	codfish
sik	seek	whitefish

sill	**sil**	herring
slätvar	**slait**vaar	brill
strömming	**strur**ming	Baltic herring, smelts
vitling	**vit**ling	whiting
ål	oal	eel

Sweden has an extensive coastline and many lakes, so it's not surprising that fish plays a major part in the country's diet. On the west coast the specialities are shellfish, fresh mackerel and cod. In the south and east, look for fresh herring, Baltic herring and whitefish. Northern Sweden features river trout and salmon, plus a distinctive small red fish, the char—*röding*.

As for herring—the national dish—ask for *silltallrik* (**sil**tahlrik) and you'll get a sample of almost every variety available.

The crayfish season starts around August 8 and continues for about six weeks. It is taken quite seriously in Sweden, when the nights are long and the parties, floating on aquavit, run on into the twilight.

Aside from all the herring, here are a few Swedish specialities which are well worth trying:

gravlax (**graav**lahks)	salmon cured with dill, pepper, sugar and salt, served with a mustard sauce
hummer (**hew**merr)	lobster, normally served cold with mayonnaise
Janssons frestelse (**yaan**sonss **frehs**terlser)	"the temptation of Jansson"—layers of sliced potatoes, marinated sprats and onions, baked in cream
krabba (**krah**bah)	crab; sometimes served with mustard sauce
lax (**lahks**)	fresh salmon, often boiled or fried
laxöring (**lahks**urring)	salmon trout, boiled, usually served cold with sauce

lutfisk
(**lewt**fisk)

codfish, steeped in a solution of slaked lime, water and soda; served with boiled potatoes and bechamel sauce, mixed with black pepper or mustard (traditional Christmas dish)

lättrökt lax
(**leht**rürkt lahks)

lightly smoked salmon often served with creamed spinach, poached egg and lemon

löjrom med gräddfil och lök
(**lur**yrom mayd grehd-feel ok lürk)

roe from bleak, served with sour cream and chopped onion

rimmad lax med stuvad potatis
(**rimm**ad lahks mayd stewvahd potaatiss)

lightly salted salmon with creamed potatoes and dill

räkor
(**rai**kor)

pink shrimps, boiled on the trawler; served with buttered toast

sikrom med gräddfil och lök
(**seek**rom mayd grehdfeel ok lürk)

roe from whitefish, served with sour cream and chopped onion

ål
(oal)

smoked eel, a speciality in the south, where it's served with creamed potatoes; you'll probably have it with scrambled eggs in the rest of Sweden

There are many ways of preparing fish. Here are some of the ways you may want it served:

baked	**ugnsbakad**	**ewngns**baakahd
cured	**gravad**	**graa**vahd
fried	**stekt**	**stay**kt
grilled	**halstrad**	**hahl**strahd
marinated	**marinerad**	mahrinn**ay**rahd
poached	**pocherad**	posh**ay**rahd
sautéed	**smörfräst**	**smürr**fraist
smoked	**rökt**	**rürkt**
steamed	**ångkokt**	**ong**kookt

Meat

You'll find practically all the familiar meat dishes in any good restaurant, plus some intriguing new ones during the hunting season. Beef is expensive in Sweden and generally not up to the quality Britons and Americans prefer. However, you can get a steak in a luxury restaurant or grillbar. Swedes eat pork more frequently than beef.

I'd like some...	**Jag skulle vilja ha...**	yaa(g) **skewler** vilyah haa
beef/lamb	**oxkött/lamm**	**ooks**khurt/lahm
pork/veal	**gris/kalv**	greess/kahlv
biff	bif	beef steak
fläskkarré	flehskah**rāy**	loin of pork
får i kål	foar ee koal	mutton boiled with white cabbage
griskotletter	**grees**kotlehterr	pork chops
grisstek	**grees**stāyk	roast pork
kalops	kah**lops**	Swedish beef stew
kalvbräss	**kahlv**brehss	sweetbread
kalvfilé	**kahlv**fillāy	fillet of veal
kalvkotletter	**kahlv**kotlehterr	veal chops
kalvlever	**kahlv**lāyverr	calf's liver
kalvstek	**kahlv**stāyk	roast veal
korv	korv	sausage
lammbog	**lahm**bōog	shoulder of lamb
lammkotletter	**lahm**kotlehterr	lamb chops
lammsadel	**lahm**saaderl	saddle of lamb
lammstek	**lahm**stāyk	roast lamb
njure	**nyēw**rer	kidney
oxbringa	**ooks**bringah	brisket of beef
oxfilé	**ooks**fillāy	fillet of beef
oxrulader	**ooks**rewlaaderr	braised rolls of beef
oxstek	**ooks**stāyk	roast beef
ragu	rah**gēw**	ragout
revbensspjäll	**rāyv**bāynsspyehl	spare ribs
skinka	**shin**kah	ham
bräckt skinka	brehkt **shin**kah	cured ham
kokt skinka	kookt **shin**kah	boiled ham
rökt skinka	**rūrkt shin**kah	smoked ham
spädgris	spai(d)greess	sucking pig

EATING OUT

Different ways your meat might be cooked:

baked	ugnstekt	ewngnstāykt
boiled	kokt	kookt
braised	stekt i gryta	stāykt ee grēwtah
fried	stekt i panna	stāykt ee pahnah
grilled	grillat	grillaht
roasted	ugnstekt	ewngnstāykt
sautéed	brynt i smör	brēwnt ee smūrr
underdone (rare)	blodig	blōōdi(g)
medium	lagom	laagom
well-done	genomstekt	yāynomstāykt

Swedish specialities

bruna bönor med fläsk
(brēwnah būrnoor māyd flehsk)

baked brown beans flavoured with vinegar and served with thick bacon slices

dillkött
(dilkhurt)

veal in a lemon and dill sauce

fläskpannkaka
(flehskpahnkaakah)

thick oven-baked pancake with bacon, served with cranberries

kåldolmar
(koaldolmahr)

stuffed cabbage with cream sauce

köttbullar
(khurtbewlahr)

meatballs, served with gravy or a brown cream sauce, and cranberries

lövbiff
(lūrvbif)

thinly-sliced beef fried with onions and served with boiled potatoes

pepparrotskött
(pehpahrrōōtskhurt)

boiled beef with horseradish sauce

pytt i panna
(pewt ee pahnah)

chunks of meat, sausages and fried potatoes topped with a fried egg, often served with pickled beetroot

sjömansbiff
(shūrmahnsbif)

beef, onion and potato casserole stewed in beer

slottsstek
(slotsstāyk)

pot roast with anchovies, brandy and syrup

Game and fowl

During the autumn hunting season you'll find game and fowl on Swedish restaurant menus. Some varieties —capercaille, black grouse, ptarmigan and hazel-hen— may be new to you. Try them!

I'd like some game.	**Jag skulle vilja ha en vilträtt.**	yaa(g) skewler vilyah haa ehn viltreht
I'd like some fowl.	**Jag skulle vilja ha fågel.**	yaa(g) skewler vilyah haa foagerl
björnstek	byūr**r**nstayk	roast bear
fasan	fahssaan	pheasant
hare	haarer	hare
järpe	yǣrper	hazel-hen
orre	orrer	black grouse
rapphöna	rahphūrnah	partridge
ren	rāyn	reindeer
renbog	rāynbōog	shoulder of reindeer
rensadel	rāynsaaderl	saddle of reindeer
renskav	rāynskaav	dried leg of reindeer, thinly sliced
renstek	rāynstayk	roast reindeer
torkat renkött	torkaht rāynkhurt	dried fillet of reindeer, thinly sliced
ripa	reepah	ptarmigan
rådjur	roayēwr	venison
rådjurssadel	roayēw**r**ssaaderl	saddle of venison
rådjursstek	roayēw**r**sstayk	roast venison
tjäder	khaiderr	capercaille
älg	ehly	elk
älgfilé	ehlyfillāy	fillet of elk
älgstek	ehlystayk	roast elk
kyckling	khew**k**ling	chicken
gås	goass	goose

Some game dishes are cooked with juniper berries and served with an exceptionally rich sauce. Vegetables, chestnuts and fruit jellies are also served with them. If you happen to be in Sweden on November 11, join in the celebration of *Mårten gås* and eat black soup and goose.

EATING OUT

Vegetables

Sweden's harsh winter climate means that imported, canned, frozen or greenhouse vegetables are all that's available most of the year. But in the brief northern summer (June, July and August) the profusion of fresh, home-grown vegetables intoxicates the Swedes. It's the time to fill up your plate with delicious artichokes, asparagus and new potatoes.

What vegetables do you recommend?	**Vilka grönsaker föreslår ni?**	vilkah grürnsaakerr fürrersloar nee
I'd prefer some salad.	**Jag skulle hellre vilja ha en sallad.**	yaa(g) skewler hehlrer vilyah haa ehn sahlahd
blandade grön-saker	**blahndahder grürn-saaker**	mixed vegetables
blomkål	**bloom**koal	cauliflower
brysselkål	**brews**serlkoal	brussels sprouts
bönor	**bür**noor	beans
grönkål	**grürn**koal	kale
gurka	**gewr**kah	cucumber
haricots verts	hahrikko vær	green beans
kronärtskocka	kroonær^tskokkah	artichoke
lök	lürk	onions
röd/gul	rürd/gewl	red/yellow
morötter	**moo**rurterr	carrots
persilja	pæ^rsilyah	parsley
potatis	po**taa**tiss	potatoes
mandelpotatis	**mahn**derlpotaatiss	high quality potatoes
purjolök	**pewr**yolürk	leeks
ris	reess	rice
rotmos	**root**mööss	mashed turnips
rädisor	**reh**dissoor	radishes
rödbetor	**rürd**baytoor	beetroot
rödkål	**rürd**koal	red cabbage
sallad	**sah**lahd	salad
sparris	**spah**riss	asparagus
spenat	speh**naat**	spinach
svamp	svahmp	mushrooms
tomater	tom**maa**terr	tomatoes
vitkål	**veet**koal	white cabbage
vitlök	**veet**lürk	garlic
ärtor	æ^rtoor	peas

Sauces

Quite a few French sauces—such as hollandaise and béarnaise—have been borrowed by Swedish cooks. But here are some which are typically Swedish:

dillsås (dilsoass)	meat broth with quantities of chopped dill
gräddfil (grehdfeel)	sour cream
gräddsås (grehdsoass)	cream sauce
löksås (lūrksoass)	brown sauce and chopped onions
peparrotssås (pehpahrrootssoass)	bechamel sauce with horseradish
persiljesmör (pæ‾silyersmurr)	parsley butter
senapssås (sāynahpssoass)	oil, vinegar, spices, sugar, dill and mustard
skarpsås (skahrpsoass)	piquant mustard sauce
sky (shew)	gravy
viltsås (viltsoass)	game sauce
vitlökssmör (veetlūrkssmurr)	garlic butter
vit sås (veet soass)	white sauce (bechamel)

Dressing

The most common salad dressing in Sweden is made of oil, vinegar, salt and pepper; on the menu it's called "French dressing". For seafood cocktails, the sauce is likely to be made of mayonnaise, ketchup and sour cream.

Cheese

While cheese in Sweden is far from being such a highly developed institution as travellers will have found it to be in, say, France, the local products are by no means insignificant. Ranging from the hard to the soft, from the bland to the pungent, the indigenous cheeses described below will certainly provide the cheese-lover's palate with adequate titillation. (And on a platter of assorted cheeses you will also find such imported classics as camembert, gorgonzola or cream cheese.)

getost
(yāytoost)
a soft, rather sweet, goat's milk cheese

herrgårdsost
(hærgoaʳdsoost)
semi-hard cheese with a strong nutty flavour; the full-cream variety resembles emmenthal, while the half-cream is similar to edam or gouda

hushållsost
(hēwssholsoost)
typical tangy farmhouse cheese

kryddost
(krewdoost)
firm, strong, semi-dry cheese with caraway seeds

mesost
(māyssoost)
amber-coloured, sweet whey cheese; definitely an acquired taste

mjukost
(myēwkoost)
soft white cheese, extremely bland

prästost
(prehstoost)
cow's milk cheese

smältost
(smehltoost)
very mild, soft, runny cheese, mostly used in cooking

sveciaost
(svāyssiahoost)
most popular Swedish cheese, semi-hard with small holes; often spiced

västerbottenost
(vehsterrbotternoost)
hard, pungent cheese from the north of Sweden

västgötaost
(vehshyūrtahoost)
aromatic, semi-hard cheese from West Gothland, sharp when mature

Fruit

Because of the climate, most Swedish fruit is imported. But there are apples, pears and plums in season, along with summer berries in abundance. Arctic cloudberries are a special delicacy—fresh or in jam, often served with ice-cream. If you have a chance, try *möjagubbar*—strawberries from the Stockholm archipelago.

Do you have fresh fruit?	**Har ni färsk frukt?**	haar nee fæ^rsk frewkt
I'd like a fruit salad.	**Jag skulle vilja ha en fruktsallad.**	yaa(g) **skewler** vilyah haa ehn **frewkt**sahlahd

ananas	ahnahnahss	pineapple
apelsin	ahperlssen	orange
aprikos	ahprikkooss	apricot
banan	bahnaan	banana
bigarråer	biggahroaerr	whitehearts
björnbär	byūr^rnbær	blackberries
blåbär	bloabær	bilberries
grapefrukt	graypfrewkt	grapefruit
hallon	hahlon	raspberries
hjortron	yoo^rtron	arctic cloudberries
jordgubbar	yōō^rdgewbahr	strawberries
krusbär	krewssbær	gooseberries
körsbär	khur^rssbær	cherries
lingon	lingon	cranberries
persika	pæ^rssikah	peach
päron	pæron	pear
smultron	smewltron	wild strawberries
vinbär	veenbær	currants
röda	rūrdah	red
svarta	svah^rtah	black
vita	veetah	white
vindruvor	veendrēwvoor	grapes
blå	bloa	blue
gröna	grūrnah	green
äpple	ehpler	apple

Dessert

And, if you've still hungry…

| I'd like a dessert, please. | **Jag skulle vilja ha en efterrätt.** | yaa(g) skewler vilyah haa ehn ehftreht |
| Something light, please. | **Någonting lätt, tack.** | noagonting leht tahk |

citronfromage	sitroonfrommaash	lemon mousse
glass	glahss	ice-cream
jordgubbsglass	yoo**r**dgewbsglahss	strawberry
pistaschglass	pistaashglahss	pistachio
hjortron	yoo**r**tron	arctic cloudberries
med vaniljglass	mayd vahnilyglahss	with vanilla ice-cream
med vispgrädde	mayd vispgrehder	with whipped cream
jordgubbar	yoo**r**dgewbahr	strawberries
med grädde	mayd grehder	with cream
med vaniljglass	mayd vahnilyglahss	with vanilla ice-cream
marängsviss	mahrehngsviss	meringues with whipped cream and chocolate sauce
melon med blåbär och hallon	mehloon mayd bloabær ok hahlon	slice of melon with bilberries and raspberries
pannkakor med vispgrädde och sylt	pahnkaakoor mayd vispgrehder ok sewlt	pancakes with whipped cream and jam
rabarberkompott	rahbahrberrkompot	stewed rhubarb
smultron med grädde	smewltron mayd grehder	wild strawberries with cream
syltomelett	sewltom(er)leht	sweet omelet with jam
tårta	toa**r**tah	layer cake
frukttårta	frewkttoa**r**tah	fruit cake
gräddtårta	grehdtoa**r**tah	cake with whipped cream
toscatårta	toskahtoa**r**tah	cake with caramel glaze
våfflor med grädde och sylt	vofloor mayd grehder ok sewlt	waffles with whipped cream and jam
äppelkaka med vaniljsås	ehperlkaakah mayd vahnilysoass	apple cake with vanilla custard

The bill (check)

A service charge is automatically added to restaurant bills. If you feel you have been very well served, add an extra tip.

I'd like to pay.	Kan jag få notan, tack.	kahn yaa(g) foa nōōtahn tahk
We'd like to pay separately.	Vi vill betala var och en för sig.	vee vil bertaalah vaar ok ehn fūrr say
Is service included?	Är dricksen inräknad?	ǣr driksern inraiknahd
You've made a mistake in this bill, I think.	Jag tror ni har gjort ett litet fel här.	yaa(g) trōōr nee haar yōō°t eht leetert fāyl hǣr
What is this amount for?	Vad står den här summan för?	vaa(d) stoar dehn hǣr sewmahn fūrr
Do you accept traveller's cheques?	Tar ni emot resechecker?	taar nee ehmōōt rāysserkhehkerr
Thank you, this is for you.	Tack, det här är för er.	tahk dāy(t) hǣr ǣr fūrr āyr
Keep the change.	Behåll växeln.	berhol vehkserln
That was a very good meal.	Det var en utsökt måltid.	dāy(t) vaar ehn ēwtsūrkt moalteed
We enjoyed it, thank you.	Vi uppskattade det mycket - tusen tack.	vee ewpskahtahder dāy(t) mewker(t) - tēwssern tahk

> **SERVERINGSAVGIFT INRÄKNAD**
> SERVICE INCLUDED

Complaints

But perhaps you'll have something to complain about:

That's not what I ordered. I asked for...	Jag beställde inte det här. Jag bad om...	yaa(g) berstehlder inter dāy(t) hǣr. yaa(g) baa(d) om
May I change this?	Kan jag få byta ut det här?	kahn yaa(g) foa bēwtah ēwt dāy(t) hǣr

The meat is...	Köttet är...	khurtert ǣr
overdone	för hårt stekt	furr hoaʳt stäykt
underdone	inte tillräckligt genomstekt	inter tilrehklit yāynomstäykt
too tough	för segt	furr sāygt
This is too...	Detta är för...	dehtah ǣr furr
bitter/salty/sweet	beskt/salt/sött	behskt/sahlt/surt
The food is cold.	Maten är kall.	maatern ǣr kahl
This isn't fresh.	Det här är inte färskt.	dāy(t) hǣr ǣr inter fæʳfskt
What's taking you so long?	Varför tar det så lång tid?	vahrfurr taar dāy(t) soa long teed
Where are our drinks?	Vad har hänt med vår beställning?	vaa(d) haar hehnt māyd voar berstehlning
This isn't clean.	Det här är inte rent.	dāy(t) hǣr ǣr inter rāynt
Would you ask the head waiter to come over?	Skulle ni vilja be hovmästaren komma hit?	skewler nee vilyah bāy hoavmehstahrern kommah heet

Drinks

The Swedish government maintains strict control over the sale of alcohol. You have to go to a special state shop, *Systembolaget* (sewst**aym**boolaagert), to buy liquor or strong beer. Very high taxes make most alcoholic beverages extremely expensive in Sweden, though wine is an exception. If money is no object, you can get almost any kind of drink in the world.

Beer

The most popular drink in Sweden is beer. The strongest brew is called *starköl,* categorized as class III. The lowest alcohol content—class I—is called *lättöl* (leht**ūr**l). If you want a bitter beer, ask for a *Pripps Blå* (pripps bloa) or a *TT Export;* for something mild, the Swedish *Falcon* or a Danish beer.

Aquavit

The national drink is served ice-cold in small glasses, to go with the smörgåsbord or an appetizer. As *snaps* (snahps) is quite strong, it's often washed down with beer. Many kinds of aquavit are flavoured with spices and herbs.

Here are a few popular types of Swedish aquavit:

Bäsk (behsk)	bitter-tasting aquavit, flavoured with wormwood
Herrgårdsbrännvin (hærgoaʳdsbrehnvin)	flavoured with caraway and whisky, matured in sherry-barrels.
Renat (rāynat)	colourless, unspiced
Skåne (skoaner)	flavoured with caraway, aniseed and fennel
Svart vinbärsbrännvin (svahʳt **veen**bæʳs-brehnvin)	aquavit, spiced with blackcurrents
Överstebrännvin (ūʳveh ʳsterbrehnvin)	flavoured with caraway

Warning: Aquavit contains about 40 per cent pure alcohol. Note that you have to state whether you want a glass of 2, 4, 6 or 8 centilitres (1 cl. = 1/3 oz.).

Glögg

Around Christmastide the Swedes drink a sweet, hot punch called *glögg* (glurg). It contains red wine, sugar, cloves, cinnamon, nuts, raisins and—watch out—pure aquavit. It warms the blood.

Punch

A popular after-dinner drink is a power-packed punch made of arrack, sugar and pure alcohol, also served warm along with the traditional Thursday pea-soup (see page 47).

Wine

Sweden imports wine from France, Italy, Spain, Algeria and other wine-producing countries. You'll find excellent Bordeaux and Burgundy vintages in hotels and luxury restaurants, or you can order a glass or carafe of less expensive wine in almost any restaurant.

I'd like a...of...	Jag skall be att få...	yaa(g) skahl bay aht foa
glass	ett glas...	eht glaass
carafe	en karaff...	ehn kahrahf
half bottle	en halv flaska...	ehn hahlv flahskah
bottle	en flaska...	ehn flahskah
I want a bottle of white/red wine.	Jag skall be att få en flaska vitt/rött vin.	yaa(g) skahl bay aht foa ehn flahskah vit/rurt veen
Do you have open wine?	Har ni något öppet vin?	haar nee noagot urpert veen

If you enjoyed the wine, you may want to say:

| Please bring me another... | Jag skall be att få ...till. | yaa(g) skahl bay aht foa...til |
| Where does this wine come from? | Varifrån kommer det här vinet? | vaarifroan kommerr day(t) hær veenert |

red	rött	rurt
white	vitt	vit
rosé	rosé	rossay
very dry	mycket torrt	mewker(t) to\rt
dry	torrt	to\rt
sweet	sött	surt
light	lätt	leht
full-bodied	fylligt	fewlit
sparkling	mousserande	moossayrahnder
chilled	kylt	khewlt
at room temperature	rumstempererat	rewmstehmperrayraht

Other alcoholic drinks

In Swedish bars and restaurants you can get almost all the drinks you're accustomed to at home. The customary international titles are used and the drinks are mixed the same way.

I'd like...	**Jag skulle vilja ha...**	yaa(g) **skew**ler vilyah haa
beer	**öl**	ūrl
Bourbon	**Bourbon**	boor**bon**
cognac	**konjak**	**kon**yahk
dry martini	**dry martini**	dry mah^r**teeni**
gin	**gin**	yin
gin-fizz	**gin-fizz**	yin-fiss
gin and tonic	**gin och tonic**	yin ok **tonnik**
port	**portvin**	poa^rtveen
rum	**rom**	rom
scotch	**skotsk whisky**	skotsk **wiski**
sherry	**sherry**	**sheh**ri
vermouth	**vermouth**	**vær**moot
(sweet/dry)	**(söt/torr)**	(sūrt/tor)
vodka	**vodka**	**vod**kah
whisky	**whisky**	**wiski**

glass	**ett glas**	eht glaass
bottle	**en flaska**	ehn **flah**skah
neat	**ren**	rāȳn
on the rocks	**med is**	māȳd eess
with water	**med vatten**	māȳd **vah**tern
with sodawater	**med sodavatten**	māȳd **sōō**dahvahtern

Of course, you don't have to order hard liquor in a bar. If you prefer, ask for juice or a soft drink:

I'd like a lemonade.	**Jag skulle vilja ha en läsk.**	yaa(g) **skew**ler vilyah haa ehn lehsk

> **SKÅL!**
> CHEERS!

Other beverages

(hot) chocolate	**(varm) choklad**	(vahrm) sho**klaa(d)**
coffee	**kaffe**	**kah**fer
cup of coffee	**en kopp kaffe**	ehn kohp **kah**fer
coffee with cream	**kaffe med grädde**	**kah**fer māȳd **greh**der
espresso coffee	**espresso**	eh**spreh**sso
fruit juice	**juice**	yōōss
apple/grapefruit	**äpple/grapefrukt**	**ehp**ler/**grayp**frewkt
lemon/orange	**citron/apelsin**	si**trōōn**/ahper**lsseen**
pineapple/tomato	**ananas/tomat**	**ah**nahnahss/**tom**maat
milk	**mjölk**	myurlk
mineral water	**mineralvatten**	minne**rraal**vahtern
orangeade	**apelsinläsk**	ahper**lsseen**lehsk
squash	**apelsinsaft**	ahper**lsseen**sahft
tea	**te**	tāȳ
with milk/lemon	**med mjölk/citron**	māȳd myurlk/si**trōōn**
iced tea	**iste**	**ees**stāȳ
tonic water	**tonic**	**ton**nik

Eating light—Snacks

I'll have one of those, please.	**Jag skall be att få en av de där, tack.**	yaa(g) skahl bāȳ aht foa ehn aav deh dǟr tahk
Please give me a/an/ some...	**Kan jag få...tack.**	kahn yaa(g) foa...tahk
biscuits (Br.)	**småkakor**	**smoa**kaakoor
bread	**bröd**	brürd
butter	**smör**	smürr
cake	**en tårta**	ehn **toar**tah
candy	**sötsaker**	**sürt**saakerr
chocolate bar	**en chokladkaka**	ehn sho**klaa(d)**kaakah
cookies	**småkakor**	**smoa**kaakoor
Danish pastry	**wienerbröd**	**wee**nerrbrürd
frankfurter	**en varm korv**	ehn **vahrm** korv
ginger snaps	**pepparkakor**	**peh**pahrkaakoor
hot-dog	**en varm korv med bröd**	ehn vahrm korv māȳd brürd
ice-cream	**en glass**	ehn glahss
pastry	**en bakelse**	ehn **baa**kerlser
roll	**en småfranska**	ehn **smoa**frahnskah
sandwich	**en smörgås**	ehn **smurr**goass
sweets	**sötsaker**	**sürt**saakerr
How much is that?	**Hur mycket kostar det?**	hēȳwr **mew**ker(t) **kos**tahr dāȳ(t)

Travelling around

Plane

Let's be very brief—because at any of the 25 domestic airports you're almost certain to find someone who speaks English.

When's the next plane to Malmö?	**När går nästa plan till Malmö?**	nǣr goar **neh**stah plaan til **mahl**mur
Is it a non-stop flight?	**Går det nonstop?**	goar dāȳ(t) **non**stop
Do I have to change planes?	**Måste jag byta plan?**	**mos**ter yaa(g) **bēw**tah plaan
I'd like a ticket to Luleå.	**Jag skulle vilja ha en biljett till Luleå.**	yaa(g) **skew**ler **vil**yah haa ehn bil**yeht** til **lēw**leroa
What's the fare to Karlstad?	**Vad kostar en biljett till Karlstad?**	vaa(d) **kos**tahr ehn bil**yeht** til **kaal**staa(d)
single (one-way)	**enkel**	**ehn**kerl
return (roundtrip)	**tur och retur**	tewr ok rer**tewr**
economy/first class	**turistklass/första klass**	tew**rist**klahss/**fur**'stah klahss
Is there an excursion fare?	**Finns det någon resa med nedsatt pris?**	finss dāȳ(t) **noa**gon **rāȳ**ssah māȳ(d) **nāȳd**sahtt preess
What time does the plane take off?	**Hur dags avgår planet?**	hewr dahgss **aav**goar **plaa**nert
What time do I have to check in?	**Hur dags måste jag checka in bagaget?**	hewr dahgss **mos**ter yaa(g) **khehk**ah in bah**gaa**shert
What's the flight number?	**Vad är flyg-numret?**	vaa(d) ǣr **flēw**gnewm-rert
What time do we arrive?	**Hur dags landar vi?**	hewr dahgss **lahn**dahr vee

<table>
<tr><td>

ANKOMST
ARRIVAL

</td><td>

AVGÅNG
DEPARTURE

</td></tr>
</table>

TRAVELLING AROUND

Train

Swedish trains are extremely comfortable—in fact, travelling second class in Sweden is often as luxurious as
first class in many other countries. Some second-class
carriages have special compartments for mothers with
infants. On long-distance trains there is usually a buffet
car.

Types of trains

Snälltåg/Expresståg (**snehl**toag/ehks- **prehs**toag)	long-distance train with luxury coaches; reservations (*platsbiljett*— **plahts**bilyeht) required
Lokaltåg (**lok**kaaltoag)	local train, stopping at all stations
Rälsbuss (**rehls**bewss)	small diesel train used on short runs
Sovvagn (**soa**vahngn)	sleeping-car
Liggplatsvagn (**lig**plahtsvahngn)	couchette (berth with blankets and pillow)
Restaurangvagn (rehs**torrahng**vahngn)	dining-car
Bagagevagn (bah**gaash**vahngn)	guard's van (baggage car)

Bus

A cheap, comfortable way to travel is by express bus.
These buses operate between major towns in the southern
and central parts of Sweden and between the capital
and coastal towns further north. A postal bus provides
an extension to the rail network and carries the mail
along with passengers in the northern region. You'll also
find package tours organized aboard luxury coaches.

Note: Most of the phrases on the following pages can
be used or adapted for bus travel.

To the railway station

Where's the railway station?	**Var ligger järn-vägsstationen?**	vaar liggerr yǟ**r**nvaigs-stahshōōnern
Taxi, please!	**Taxi!**	tahksi
Take me to the railway station.	**Till järnvägssta-tionen, tack.**	til yǟ**r**nvaigsstah-shōōnern tahk
What's the fare?	**Hur mycket kostar det?**	hēwr mewker(t) kostahr dāy(t)

INGÅNG	ENTRANCE
UTGÅNG	EXIT
TILL SPÅREN	TO THE PLATFORMS

Where's the...?

Where is/are the...?	**Var är...?**	vaar ǟr
baggage check	**resgods-inlämningen**	rāysgoods-inlehmningern
barber's	**frisören**	frissürrern
booking office	**biljettkontoret**	bilyehtkontōōrert
buffet	**byffén**	bewfāyn
currency-exchange office	**växelkontoret**	vehkserlkontōōrert
information office	**informations-disken**	informahshōōns-diskern
inquiry office	**informations-disken**	informahshōōns-diskern
left-luggage office	**resgodsinläm-ningen**	rāysgoodsinlehm-ningern
lost-property office (lost-and-found)	**hittegods-inlämningen**	hittergoodsinlehm-ningern
luggage lockers	**väskförvarings-facken**	vehskfurrvaarings-fahkern
news-stand	**tidningskiosken**	tee(d)ningskhioskern
platform 7	**spår 7**	spoar 7
reservations office	**biljettkontoret**	bilyehtkontōōrert
restaurant	**restaurangen**	rehstorrahngern
ticket office	**biljettluckan**	bilyehtlewkahn
toilets	**toaletterna**	tooahlehte**r**nah
waiting room	**väntsalen**	vehntsaalern

FOR TAXI, see page 27

TRAVELING AROUND

TURISTBYRÅ	TOURIST INFORMATION
UTLÄNDSK VALUTA	CURRENCY EXCHANGE

Inquiries

In Sweden [i] means information office.

When is the...train to Uppsala?	**Hur dags går...tåg till Uppsala?**	hewr dahgss goar...toag til ewpsaalah
first/last/next	**första/sista/nästa**	furrstah/sistah/ nehstah
What's the fare to Örebro?	**Vad kostar biljetten till Örebro?**	vaa(d) kostahr bilyehtern til urrerbroo
Is it a through train?	**Är det ett snälltåg?**	ær day(t) eht snehltoag
What time does the train arrive at Helsingborg?	**Hur dags ankommer tåget till Helsingborg?**	hewr dahgss ahnkommerr toagert til hehlsingbory
Is there a dining-car on the train?	**Finns det restaurangvagn på tåget?**	finss day(t) rehstorrahngvahngn poa toagert
Is there a sleeping-car on the train?	**Finns det sovvagn på tåget?**	finss day(t) soavahngn poa toagert
Does the train stop at Norrköping?	**Stannar tåget i Norrköping?**	stahnahr toagert ee norkhurping
What platform does the train for Malmö leave from?	**Från vilket spår avgår tåget till Malmö?**	froan vilkert spoar aavgoar toagert til mahlmur
I'd like to buy a timetable.	**Jag skulle vilja köpa en tidtabell.**	yaa(g) skewler vilyah khurpah ehn teedtahbehl

Note: Children travel free on trains, buses and underground up to the age of six. Between six and 12 they pay half fare. People of 65 and over (foreigners as well) benefit from a 50% reduction. A special card is required and can be obtained through any travel bureau or at railway stations.

Det är ett snälltåg.	It's a through train.
Ni måste byta i...	You have to change at...
Spår...är...	Platform...is...
därborta/uppför trappan/ nerför trappan	over there/upstairs/ downstairs
till vänster/till höger	on the left/on the right
Det går ett tåg till... kl...	There's a train to... at...
Ert tåg avgår från spår...	Your train will leave from platform... ,
Det kommer att vara... minuter försenat.	There'll be a delay of... minutes.

Tickets

I want a ticket to Lund.	Jag skall be att få en biljett till Lund.	yaa(g) skahl bay aht foa ehn bilyeht til lewnd
single (one-way)	enkel	ehnkerl
return (roundtrip)	tur och retur	tewr ok rertewr
first class	första klass	fur^rstah klahss
second class	andra klass	ahndrah klahss
Is there a rebate for pensioners/ students?	Får pensionärer/ studenter rabatt?	foar pahnshonnäärerr/ stewdehnterr rahbaht
I'd like to reserve a seat.	Jag skall be att få beställa en plats.	yaa(g) skahl bay aht foa berstehlah ehn plahtss

Första eller andra klass?	First or second class?
Enkel eller tur och retur?	Single or return (one-way or roundtrip)?
Rökare/icke rökare?	Smoker/non-smoker?
Fönsterplats/plats vid mittgången?	Window seat/aisle seat?
Hur gammal är han/hon?	How old is he/she?

TRAVELLING AROUND

All aboard...

Is this the right platform for the train to Luleå?	Är det här rätt spår för tåget till Luleå?	ǣr dāȳ(t) hǣr reht spoar furr **toa**gert til **lēw**leroa
Is this the right train to Östersund?	Går det här tåget till Östersund?	goar dāȳ(t) hǣr **toa**gert til urster**'sewnd**
Excuse me. May I get by?	Förlåt. Kan jag få komma förbi?	furr**'loat**. kahn yaa(g) foa **komm**ah furr**bee**
Is this seat taken?	Är den här platsen upptagen?	ǣr dehn hǣr **plaht**-sern **ewp**taagern

---

RÖKNING FÖRBJUDEN
NO SMOKING

I think that's my seat.	Jag tror att det där är min plats.	yaa(g) trōȯr aht dāȳ(t) dǣr ǣr min plahtss
Would you let me know before we get to Jönköping?	Skulle ni kunna säga till mig innan vi kommer till Jönköping?	**skew**ler nee **kewn**nah **seh**yah til may **inn**ahn vee **komm**err til yurnk**hū̄r**ping
What station is this?	Vilken station är det här?	**vilk**en stah**shōōn** ǣr dāȳ(t) hǣr
How long does the train stop here?	Hur länge stannar tåget här?	hēwr **lehng**er **stahn**nahr **toa**gert hǣr
When do we get to Kiruna?	När kommer vi till Kiruna?	nǣr **komm**err vee til **kirr**ewnah

Sometime on the journey the ticket-collector (*konduktören* –– kondewk**tū̄r**rern) will come around and say: *Biljetterna, tack!* (Tickets, please!).

Eating

If you want a full meal in the dining-car *(restaurang-vagn)*, you may have to get a ticket in advance. There are usually two sittings for each meal. Tell the attendant which one you prefer. On shorter runs you can buy coffee, beer, soft drinks, sandwiches and cakes from a steward aboard the train.

| First/second sitting for dinner. | Första/andra serveringen. | fur**r**stah/**ah**ndrah særv**ay**ringern |
| Where's the dining-car? | Var är restaurang-vagnen? | vaar **a**̈r rehstorr**ah**ng-vahngnern |

Sleeping

Are there any free compartments in the sleeping-car?	Finns det några lediga kupéer i sovvagnen?	finss d**ay**(t) **no**agrah **lay**diggah kewp**ay**err ee **so**avahngnern
Where's the sleeping-car?	Var är sovvagnen?	vaar **a**̈r **so**avahngnern
Where's my berth?	Vilken är min bädd?	**vil**kern **a**̈r min behd
Compartments...and ..., please.	Kupéer...och..., tack.	kewp**ay**err...ok... tahk
I'd like an upper/lower berth.	Jag skall be att få en överbädd/underbädd.	yaa(g) skahl b**ay** aht foa ehn **u**̈rverrbehd/ **ewn**derrbehd
Would you make up our berths?	Skulle ni kunna göra i ordning våra bäddar?	**skew**ler nee **kew**nah **yu**̈rrah ee o**r**dning voarah behdahr
Would you call me at 7 o'clock?	Skulle ni kunna väcka mig kl. 7?	**skew**ler nee **kew**nah **veh**kah may klokkahn 7
Would you bring me some coffee/tea in the morning?	Skulle jag kunna få lite kaffe/te i morgon bitti?	**skew**ler yaa(g) **kew**nah foa **lee**ter kahfer/t**ay** ee morron **bit**ti

Baggage and porters

| Can you help me with my bags? | Skulle ni kunna hjälpa mig med mitt bagage? | **skew**ler nee **kew**nah yehlpah may m**ay**d mit bah**gaa**sh |
| Please put them down here. | Var snäll och ställ ner det här. | vaar snehl ok stehl n**ay**r d**ay**(t) h**a**̈r |

If you wish, you may send your luggage by *polletering* (poller**tay**ring)—registered in the guard's van (baggage car), to be collected at the end of the trip. There's an extra charge.

FOR PORTERS, see also page 24

TRAVELLING AROUND

Lost!

We hope you'll have no need for the following phrases on your trip...but just in case:

Where's the lost-property office (lost-and-found)?	**Var är hittegods-inlämningen?**	vaar ær hittergoods-inlehmningern
I've lost my...	**Jag har förlorat mitt...**	yaa(g) haar fur'looraht mit
this morning	**i morse**	ee mo'ser
yesterday	**i går**	ee goar
I lost it in...	**Jag tappade det i/på...**	yaa(g) tahpahder dāy(t) ee/poa
It's very valuable.	**Det är mycket värdefullt.**	dāy(t) ær mewker(t) vær'derfewlt

Underground (subway)

Stockholm's *Tunnelbana* is the equivalent of the London Underground or the New York Subway. Lines extend from the centre of the city to the suburbs.* Maps of the entire system are displayed inside every station and aboard every train. Pocket maps may also be obtained from newsagents and travel agents. Underground stations are marked with a blue "T". Services begin at 5 a.m. and continue until midnight; reduced service continues late into the night on some lines.

Where's the nearest underground station?	**Var ligger när-maste tunnel-banestation?**	vaar liggerr nærmahster tewnerlbaaner-stahshoon
Does this train go to the Central Station?	**Går det här tåget till Centralen?**	goar dāy(t) hær toagert til sehntraalern
Is the next station Hornstull?	**Är nästa station Hornstull?**	ær nehstah stahshoon hoo'nstewl

* In many cases, the cheapest way to get around is to buy a booklet of coupons. The minimum fare is the equivalent of two coupons. Between 10 a.m. and 3 p.m. a single ticket is also valid for a two-way trip.

Bus

Get your ticket from the driver when you board the bus. You can transfer from bus to underground on the same ticket, which is valid for one hour. In major cities it's worthwhile buying a booklet of tickets at a reduced price if you plan to travel extensively. The fare on buses and taxis doubles after midnight.

I'd like a booklet of tickets.	Jag skulle vilja ha ett biljetthäfte.	yaa(g) skewler vilyah haa eht bilyehthehfter
Where can I get a bus to the Opera?	Varifrån går bussen till Operan?	vaarifroan goar bewssern til oop(er)rahn
Where's the bus stop/terminus?	Var är busshåll-platsen/ändsta-tionen?	vaar ær bewssshol-plahtsern/ehnd-stahshōonern
When is the...bus to Djurgården?	När går...bussen till Djurgården?	nær goar...bewssern til yēwrgoardern
first/last/next	första/sista/nästa	furrstah/sistah/nehstah
How often do the buses go to Valdemarsudde?	Hur ofta går bussarna till Valdemarsudde?	hēwr oftah goar bewssahrnah til vahldermahrsewder
How much is the fare to Gröna Lund?	Hur mycket kostar det till Gröna Lund?	hēwr mewker(t) kostahr dāy(t) til grūrnah lewnd
Do I have to change buses?	Måste jag byta buss?	moster yaa(g) bēwtah bewss
Is this a transfer ticket?	Är detta en över-gångsbiljett?	ær dehtah ehn ūrverr-gongsbilyeht
How long does the journey take?	Hur lång tid tar resan?	hēwr long teed taar rāyssahn
Will you tell me when to get off?	Kan ni säga till mig när jag skall gå av?	kahn nee sehyah til may nær yaa(g) skahl goa aav

| BUSSHÅLLPLATS | REGULAR BUS STOP |
| STANNAR PÅ BEGÄRAN | STOPS ON REQUEST |

| Please let me off at the next stop. | **Var snäll och låt mig gå av vid nästa hållplats.** | vaar snehl ok loat may goa aav veed nehstah holplahtss |
| May I please have my luggage? | **Kan jag få mitt bagage, tack?** | kahn yaa(g) foa mit bah**gaash**, tahk |

Boats

Regular boat and ferry services link Sweden's islands with the mainland. Ferryboats between Sweden and Denmark carry trains and cars as well as passengers. Steamer trips on Sweden's lakes and waterways offer beautiful sightseeing opportunities.

An added incentive to travel by boat between Sweden and other countries is the vastly reduced price of alcoholic beverages on board once you reach international waters!

Other modes of transport

Cycling is a popular pastime in Sweden, in the cities as well as the countryside. You may rent a machine at a bicycle shop.

bicycle	**cykel**	sewkerl
boat	**båt**	boat
canoe	**kanot**	kah**noot**
houseboat	**husbåt**	hewsboat
motorboat	**motorbåt**	mootorboat
rowing boat	**roddbåt**	roodboat
sailing boat	**segelbåt**	saygerlboat
helicopter	**helikopter**	hehli**kop**terr
hitchhiking	**liftning**	liftning
horseriding	**ridning**	reedning
moped	**moped**	mopayd
motorcycle	**motorcykel**	mooto'sewkerl

And if you're really stuck, start...

| walking | **promenera** | prommer**nay**rah |

Around and about—Sightseeing

Here we're more concerned with the cultural aspect of
life than with entertainment; and, for the moment, with
towns rather than the countryside. If you want a guide
book, ask...

Can you recommend a good guide book on Malmö?	**Kan ni rekommendera en bra guidebok över Malmö?**	kahn nee rehkommerndāyrah ehn braa **guide**bōok **ūr**ver **mahl**mur
Where's the tourist office?	**Var ligger turistbyrån?**	vaar **ligg**err tewrist**bew**roan
What are the main points of interest?	**Vad finns det för sevärdheter?**	vaa(d) finss dāy(t) fürr **sāy**vär'd**hāy**terr
We're here for...	**Vi är här...**	vee ær hær
only a few hours a day 3 days a week	**bara några timmar en dag 3 dagar en vecka**	baarah **noa**grah **timm**ahr ehn daa(g) 3 **daa**(gah)r ehn **vehk**ah
Can you recommend a (city) sightseeing tour?	**Kan ni rekommendera någon rundtur (i stan)?**	kahn nee rehkommerndāyrah **noa**gon rewn(d)tewr (ee staan)
Where does the bus start from?	**Varifrån startar bussen?**	vaarifroan stah'tahr **bewss**ern
Will it pick us up at the hotel?	**Hämtar den oss vid hotellet?**	**hehm**tahr dehn oss veed hotehlert
How much does the tour cost?	**Hur mycket kostar rundturen?**	hewr **mew**ker(t) **kost**ahr rewn(d)**tewr**ern
What time does the tour start?	**Hur dags startar den?**	hewr dahgss **stah**'tahr dehn
What time do we get back?	**Hur dags kommer vi tillbaka?**	hewr dahgss **komm**err vee til**baa**kah
We'd like to rent a car for the day.	**Vi skulle vilja hyra en bil för dagen.**	vee **skew**ler **vil**yah **hew**rah ehn beel fürr **daa**(ger)n
Is there an English-speaking guide?	**Finns det någon engelsktalande guide?**	finss dāy(t) **noa**gon **ehng**erlsktaalahnder guide

SIGHTSEEING

FOR TELLING THE TIME, see page 178

Where is/are the...?	Var ligger...?	vaar liggerr
amusement park	nöjesparken	nuryerspahrkern
art gallery	konstgalleriet	konstgahlerriert
artists' quarter	konstnärskvar-teren	konstnǣrs-kvahᶠtāyrern
beach	stranden	strahndern
botanical gardens	botaniska trädgården	bootaaniskah trai(d)goaᶠdern
bridge	bron	brōōn
building	byggnaden	bewgnahdern
business district	affärskvarteren	ahfǣᶠskvaᶠtāyrern
castle	slottet	slottert
cathedral	domkyrkan	doomkhewrkahn
cemetery	kyrkogården	khewrkogoaᶠdern
citadel	fästningen	fehstningern
city centre	stadscentrum	stahdssehntrewm
city hall	stadshuset	stahdshewssert
church	kyrkan	khewrkahn
concert hall	Konserthuset	konsǣrhēwssert
docks	(skepps)dockorna	(shehps)dokkooᶠnah
downtown area	stadscentrum	stahdssehntrewm
exhibition	utställningen	ēwtstehlningern
factory	fabriken	fahbreekern
fortress	borgen	boryern
fountain	fontänen	fontainern
gardens	trädgårdarna	trai(d)goaᶠdahᶠnah
harbour	hamnen	hahmnern
lake	sjön	shurn
library	biblioteket	bibliotāykert
market	torget	toryert
memorial	minnesmärket	minnersmǣrkert
monument	monumentet	monnewmehntert
museum	muséet	mewssehert
Museum of Modern Art	Moderna Muséet	moodǣᶠnah mewssehert
National Museum	Nationalmuseum	nahtshoonaal-mewssehwm
observatory	observatoriet	obsǣrvahtooriert
old city	Gamla Stan	gahmlah staan
opera house	operan	ōōp(er)rahn
palace	slottet	slottert
park	parken	pahrkern
parliament building	riksdagshuset	riksdahgshewssert
planetarium	planetariet	plahnertaariert
river	floden	floodern
Royal Palace	Kungliga Slottet	kewngliggah slottert

FOR ASKING THE WAY, see page 144

shopping centre	**shoppingcentrum**	shoppingsehntrewm
stadium	**stadion**	staadion
statue	**statyn**	stahtewn
swimming pool	**simbassängen**	simbahssehngern
synagogue	**synagogan**	sewnahgoogahn
television studios	**TV-studiorna**	tayveh-stewdio^rnah
theatre	**teatern**	tehaater^rn
tomb	**graven**	graavern
tower	**tornet**	too^rnert
town hall	**Stadshuset**	stahdshewssert
university	**universitetet**	ewnivæ^rsittaytert
Vasa Ship	**Skeppet Vasa**	shehpert vaassah
watermill	**vattenkvarnen**	vahternkvaa^rnern
zoo	**zoologiska trädgården**	soloagiskah trai(d)goa^rdern

Admission

Is...open on Sundays?	**Är...öppet på söndagar?**	ær...urpert poa surndaagahr
When does it open/ close?	**När öppnar/ stänger man?**	nær urpnahr/ stehngerr mahn
Where do I get tickets?	**Var kan jag köpa biljetter?**	vaar kahn yaa(g) khūrpah bilyehterr
How much is the entrance fee?	**Vad kostar inträdet?**	vaa(d) kostahr intraidert
Is there any reduction for pensioners/ students/children?	**Är det billigare för pensionärer/ studenter/barn?**	ær day(t) billiggahrer fürr pahnshonnærerr/ stewdehnterr/baa^rn
Have you a guide book in English?	**Har ni någon guidebok på engelska?**	haar nee noagon guidebōōk poa ehngerlskah
Can I buy a catalogue?	**Kan jag få köpa en katalog?**	kahn yaa(g) foa khūrpah ehn kahtahloag
Is it all right to take pictures?	**Är det tillåtet att fotografera?**	ær day(t) tilloatert aht fottograhfāyrah

---

FRITT INTRÄDE ADMISSION FREE

FOTOGRAFERING FÖRBJUDEN NO CAMERAS ALLOWED

SIGHTSEEING

Who—What—When?

What's that building?	**Vad är det där för byggnad?**	vaa(d) ær dāȳ(t) dǣr fūrr bewgnahd
Who was the...?	**Vem var...?**	vehm vaar
architect	**arkitekten**	ahrkhittehktern
artist	**konstnären**	konstnǣrern
painter	**målaren**	moalahrern
sculptor	**skulptören**	skewlptūrrern
Who built it?	**Vem har byggt det?**	vehm haar bewgt dāȳ(t)
Who painted that picture?	**Vem målade den där tavlan?**	vehm moalahder dehn dǣr taavlahn
When did he live?	**När levde han?**	nǣr lāȳvder hahn
When was it built?	**När byggdes det?**	nǣr bewgderss dāȳ(t)
Where's the house where...lived?	**Var ligger huset där...bodde?**	vaar liggerr hēwssert dǣr...booder
We're interested in...	**Vi är intresserade av...**	vee ǣr intrehssāȳrahder aav
antiques	**antikviteter**	ahntikvittāȳterr
archaeology	**arkeologi**	ahrkehologgi
art	**konst**	konst
botany	**botanik**	bootahneek
ceramics	**keramik**	khǣrahmeek
coins	**mynt**	mewnt
crafts	**konsthantverk**	konsthahntvǣrk
fine arts	**de sköna konsterna**	deh shūrnah konsterʳnah
folk art	**folkkonst**	folkkonst
furniture	**möbler**	mūrblerr
history	**historia**	histooriah
medicine	**medicin**	mehdersseen
modern art	**modern konst**	modǣʳn konst
natural history	**naturhistoria**	nahtēwrhistooriah
ornithology	**ornitologi**	oʳnitologgi
painting	**måleri**	moalerri
pottery	**lergods**	lāȳrgoodss
sculpture	**skulptur**	skewl(p)tewr
wild life	**djurliv**	yewrleev
zoology	**zoologi**	sologgi
Where's the... department?	**Var är avdelningen för...?**	vaar ǣr aavdaylningern furr

Just the adjective you've been looking for...

It's...	Det är...	dāy(t) ǣr
amazing	häpnadsväckande	haipnahdsvehkahnder
awful	hemskt	hehmskt
beautiful	vackert	vahkerᵗ
delightful	förtjusande	furᵏkhēwssahnder
disappointing	nedslående	nāydsloaehnder
excellent	utmärkt	ewtmærkt
gloomy	dystert	dewsterᵗ
impressive	imponerande	imponnāyrahnder
incomparable	ojämförbart	ooyehmfurrbahᵗ
interesting	intressant	intrehssahnt
mediocre	medelmåttigt	māyderlmottit
overwhelming	överväldigande	ūrverrvehldiggahnder
remarkable	enastående	āynahstoaernder
sinister	olycksbådande	ōōlewksboadahnder
strange	underligt	ewnderᵗlit
superb	storartat	stōōraaᵗtaht
terrible	fruktansvärt	frewktahnsvǣᵗt
terrifying	skrämmande	skrehmahnder
ugly	fult	fewlt

Church services

The state church of Sweden is Lutheran. But freedom of religion is assured and other denominations have their own churches.

Is there a... near here?	Finns det någon... här i närheten?	finss dāy(t) noagon hǣr ee nǣrhāytern
Catholic/ Protestant church	romersk-katolsk/ protestantisk kyrka	roomǣrsk-kahtōōlsk/ prottehstahntisk khēwrkah
synagogue	synagoga	sewnahgoogah
At what time is...?	Hur dags börjar...?	hēwr dahgss būrryahr
mass	mässan	mehssahn
the service	gudstjänsten	gewdskhainstern
Where can I find a... who speaks English?	Var kan jag få tag på en...som talar engelska?	vaar kahn yaa(g) foa taag poa ehn...som taalahr ehngerlskah
priest	katolsk präst	kahtōōlsk prehst
minister	protestantisk präst	prottehstahntisk prehst
rabbi	rabbin	rahbin

Relaxing

Cinema (movies)—Theatre

For popular films it's advisable to buy tickets in advance. All films are shown in their original language with Swedish subtitles. Generally, there are separate performances at 3, 7 and 9 p.m. No smoking is allowed in cinemas or theatres.

Advance booking is essential for theatres and the opera. Evening performances start at around 7.30 p.m. There are usually matinées on Saturdays or Sundays as well.

To find out what's playing, consult the newspapers and billboards or the weekly tourist publication in Stockholm and Gothenburg.

Have you a copy of "This Week in..."?	Har ni ett exemplar av "Denna vecka i..."?	haar nee eht ehksehmplaar aav "dehnah vehkah ee"
What's showing at the cinema tonight?	Vad går det för filmer i kväll?	vaa(d) goar day(t) furr filmerr ee kvehl
What's playing at the...Theatre?	Vad spelas på... teatern?	vaa(d) spehlahss poa...tehaater'n
What sort of play is it?	Vad är det för slags pjäs?	vaa(d) ær day(t) furr slahgss pyaiss
Who's it by?	Vem har skrivit den?	vehm haar skreevit dehn
Can you recommend a...?	Kan ni rekommendera...?	kahn nee rehkommerndayrah
good film	en bra film	ehn braa film
comedy	en komedi	ehn kommerdee
something light	någonting lättsamt	noagonting lehtsahmt
drama	ett drama	eht draamah
musical	en operett (musical)	ehn oop(er)reht mewssikkaal

revue	en revy	ehn rehvew
thriller	en kriminalfilm	ehn krimminnaalfilm
western	en Vilda Västern	ehn vildah vehster'n
Where's that new film by...being shown?	Var går den nya filmen av...?	vaar goar dehn newah filmern aav
Who's in it?	Vilka är rollinnehavarna?	vilkah är rollinnerhaavah'rnah
Who's playing the lead?	Vem har huvudrollen?	vehm haar hewvewdrollern
Who's the director?	Vem är regissör?	vehm är rehshissurr
What time does it begin/end?	Hur dags börjar/ slutar filmen?	hewr dahgss burryahr/ slewtahr filmern
What time does the first evening performance start?	Hur dags börjar första kvällsföreställningen?	hewr dahgss burryahr fur'stah kvehlsfürrerstehlningern
Are there any tickets for tonight?	Finns det några biljetter till i kväll?	finss day(t) noagrah bilyehterr til ee kvehl
How much are the tickets?	Hur mycket kostar biljetterna?	hewr mewker(t) kostahr bilyehter'nah
I want to reserve 2 tickets for the show on Friday evening.	Jag skulle vilja beställa 2 biljetter till föreställningen på fredag kväll.	yaa(g) skewler vilyah berstehlah 2 bilyehterr til fürrerstehlningern poa fraydaa(g) kvehl
Can I have a ticket for the matinée on...?	Kan jag få en biljett till matinéen på...?	kahn yaa(g) foa ehn bilyeht til mahtinnayn poa
I'd like a box for 4.	Jag skulle vilja ha en loge för 4.	yaa(g) skewler vilyah haa ehn losh fürr 4
I want a seat in the stalls (orchestra).	Jag skulle vilja ha en plats på parkett.	yaa(g) skewler vilyah haa ehn plahtss poa pahrkeht
Not too far back.	Inte för långt bak.	inter furr longt baak
Somewhere in the middle.	Någonstans i mitten.	noagonstahnss ee mittern
How much are the seats in the circle (balcony)?	Hur mycket kostar biljetterna på första raden?	hewr mewker(t) kostahr bilyehter'nah poa fur'stah raadern

RELAXING

| At what theatre is that new play by... being performed? | På vilken teater går den nya pjäsen av...? | poa vilkern tehaaterr goar dehn newah pyaissern aav |
| May I please have a programme? | Skulle jag kunna få ett program? | skewler yaa(g) kewnah foa eht proograhm |

Tyvärr är det utsålt.	I'm sorry, we're sold out.
Det finns bara några få platser kvar på...	There are only a few seats left in the...
parkett	stalls (orchestra)
balkong	circle (balcony)
Det finns bara ståplats.	There's standing room only.
Kan jag få se er biljett?	May I see your ticket?
Det här är er plats.	This is your seat.

Opera—Ballet—Concert

Where's the opera house?	Var ligger Operan?	vaar liggerr $\overline{oo}$p(er)rahn
Where's the concert hall?	Var ligger Konserthuset?	vaar liggerr konsǣr-hewssert
What's on at the opera tonight?	Vad ges på Operan i kväll?	vaa(d) yǟyss poa $\overline{oo}$p(er)rahn ee kvehl
Who's singing?	Vem sjunger?	vehm shewngerr
Who's dancing?	Vem dansar?	vehm dahnsahr
What time does the programme start?	Hur dags börjar föreställningen?	hewr dahgss burryahr fürrerstehlningern
What orchestra is playing?	Vad är det för orkester?	vaa(d) ǟr day(t) furr orkehsterr
When is the intermission?	När är det paus?	nǟr ǟr day(t) paaewss
Who's the soloist?	Vem är solist?	vehm ǟr soolist
Who's the conductor?	Vem är dirigent?	vehm ǟr dirrishehnt

Nightclubs

There are only a few nightclubs with floor shows, but you will find discotheques offering music, dancing and snacks. Membership is required for entry to some of the discotheques but this can usually be arranged on the spot.

Nightclubs are a feature of the larger towns only. In the countryside the nightlife is confined to the biggest —or often the only—hotel in town. This will be the place where people meet, with dancing once or twice a week. Note that no alcohol may be sold after midnight. Correct dress is required and a tie is compulsory.

Can you recommend a good nightclub/ cabaret?	**Kan ni rekommendera en bra nattklubb/kabaré?**	kahn nee rehkommern-dayrah ehn braa nahtklewb/ kahbahray
Is there a floor show?	**Finns det någon scenunderhållning?**	finss day(t) noagon saynewnderrholning
What time does the floor show start?	**Hur dags börjar scenunderhållningen?**	hewr dahgss burryahr saynewnderrholningern
Is a dark suit/ evening dress necessary?	**Måste man ha mörk kostym/ aftonklänning?**	moster mahn haa murrk kostewm/ ahftonklehning

And once inside...

A table for 2, please.	**Ett bord för 2, tack.**	eht boo'd furr 2 tahk
My name's...	**Mitt namn är...**	mit nahmn ær...yaa(g)
I reserved a table for 4.	**Jag har reserverat ett bord för 4.**	haar rehsserrvayraht eht boo'd furr 4
I telephoned you earlier.	**Jag ringde tidigare.**	yaa(g) ringder teediggahrer
We haven't got a reservation.	**Vi har inte beställt bord.**	vee haar inter berstehlt boo'd

Dancing

Where can we go dancing?	**Var kan vi gå och dansa?**	vaar kahn vee goa ok **dahn**sah
Is there a discotheque in town?	**Finns det något diskotek i stan?**	finss dāȳ(t) noagot diskot**āy**k ee staan
There's a dance at the...	**Det är dans på...**	dāȳ(t) ær **dahn**ss poa
Do you like to dance?	**Tycker ni om att dansa?**	**tew**kerr nee om aht **dahn**sah
May I have this dance?	**Får jag lov?**	foar yaa(g) loav
Yes, I'd love to.	**Ja, det vore trevligt.**	yaa, dāȳ(t) **voo**rer **trāȳ**vlit

Do you happen to play...?

On a rainy day, this page may solve your problems.

Do you happen to play chess?	**Spelar ni möjligtvis schack?**	**spāy**lahr nee **mur**ylitveess shahk
I'm afraid I don't.	**Nej, tyvärr inte.**	nay tewvær **in**ter
No, but I'll give you a game of draughts (checkers).	**Nej, men jag spelar gärna dam med er.**	nay mehn yaa(g) **spāy**lahr yæ**r**nah daam māȳd āȳr
king	**kung**	kewng
queen	**dam**	daam
castle (rook)	**torn**	tōō**r**n
bishop	**löpare**	**lur**pahrer
knight	**springare**	**spring**ahrer
pawn	**bonde**	**boon**der
Check!	**Schack!**	shahk
Checkmate!	**Schackmatt!**	**shahk**maht
Do you play cards?	**Spelar ni kort?**	**spāy**lahr nee koo**r**t
bridge	**bridge**	bridsh
canasta	**canasta**	kah**nah**stah
gin rummy	**gin rummy**	"gin rummy"
whist	**whist**	vist
pontoon (21)	**21**	khē**w**goeht
poker	**poker**	**poa**kerr

ace	**ess**	ehss
king	**kung**	kewng
queen	**dam**	daam
jack	**knekt**	knehkt
joker	**joker**	yoakerr
hearts	**hjärter**	yæᶠterr
diamonds	**ruter**	rewterr
clubs	**klöver**	klūᵛverr
spades	**spader**	spaaderr
no bid	**pass**	pahss

Casino and gambling

Casinos are illegal in Sweden, though some hotels run legal roulette games in summer for very small stakes, the chips only redeemable for food and drink.

Tips is the pertinent Swedish word for the football (soccer) pools. Each week 12 results are picked. Tobacconists' sell the coupons.

Well-known courses for harness racing *(trav)* are Solvalla (Stockholm) and Åby (Gothenburg) and for thoughbred racing *(galopp)*, Täby (Stockholm) and Jägersro (Malmö). There is a yearly Swedish Derby in mid July at Jägersro (for horses bred in Scandinavia).

Playing the numbers is legal in Sweden. Tobacconists' sell tickets for the monthly national lottery *(Penninglotteriet)*.

A new and rapidly burgeoning fad in Sweden is *bingo*. This popular and quite inexpensive game of chance needs no explanation to Britons and Americans. It's played in halls all over Sweden, in towns large and small. Even on board some of the steamers plying Baltic waters Kelly's eye and clickety-click now rule the waves!

FOR NUMBERS, see page 175

Sports

In summer the most popular sports in Sweden are golf, tennis, jogging, bicycling, horse-riding, swimming and sailing. In winter the Swedes are active skiers and skaters.

Where's the nearest golf course?	**Var ligger närmaste golfbana?**	vaar **l**iggerr **nær**mahster **g**olfbaanah
Can we hire (rent) clubs?	**Kan vi hyra klubbor?**	kahn vee hēwrah klewboor
Where are the tennis courts?	**Var ligger tennisbanan?**	vaar **l**iggerr **t**ehnisbaanahn
Can I hire a racket and balls?	**Kan jag hyra racket och bollar?**	kahn yaa(g) hēwrah rahkert ok **b**ollahr
Do I have to make an appointment?	**Måste jag beställa tid?**	**m**oster yaa(g) berstehlah teed
Where's the race course?	**Var ligger hästkapplöpningsbanan?**	vaar **l**iggerr **h**ehstkahplurpningsbaanahn
What's the admission charge?	**Vad kostar det i inträde?**	vaa(d) **k**ostahr dāy(t) ee intraider
Is there a swimming pool here?	**Finns det en simbassäng här?**	finss dāy(t) ehn simbahssehng hær
Is it open-air or indoors?	**Är den utomhus eller inomhus?**	ær dehn ēwtomhewss ehlerr innomhewss
Can one swim in the lake/river?	**Kan man simma i sjön/floden?**	kahn mahn simmah ee shurn/flōōdern
Is there a bowling alley/billiard hall near here?	**Finns det en bowlingbana/ett biljardrum i närheten här?**	finss dāy(t) ehn bovlingbaanah/eht bilyaardrewm ee nærhāytern hær
I'd like to see a/an...	**Jag skulle vilja se en...**	yaa(g) skewler vilyah say ehn
football match ice-hockey match boxing match	**fotbollsmatch ishockymatch boxningsmatch**	fōōtbolsmahtsh eesshokkimmahtsh booksningsmahtsh
Who's playing?	**Vilka lag spelar?**	vilkah laag spaylahr
Where can I hire a bicycle?	**Var kan jag hyra en cykel?**	vaar kahn yaa(g) hēwrah ehn sewkerl

Hiking

The northern part of Sweden—Jämtland and Lappland, for example—is best explored on foot. Many hotels organize hiking excursions. Excellent overnight huts are provided along the trails.

Can you recommend any hikes in the area of...?	**Kan ni rekommendera någon led i...trakten?**	kahn nee rehkommern-dayrah noagon layd ee...trahktern
What is the approximate distance between the overnight huts?	**Hur långt är det mellan varje vandrarhem?**	hewr longt ær day(t) mehlahn vahryer vahndrahrhehm
Where can I buy hiking equipment?	**Var kan jag köpa en vandrar-utrustning?**	vaar kahn yaa(g) khurpah ehn vahn-drahrewtrewstning
Where can I buy a rucksack?	**Var kan jag köpa en ryggsäck?**	vaar kahn yaa(g) khurpah ehn rewgsehk

Fishing

Fishing enthusiasts have the sea, lakes and rivers to occupy them. In winter, too, ice-fishing is a favourite sport. You can obtain a permit from the Tourist Office.

Is there any good fishing around here?	**Är det bra fiske-vatten i trakten?**	ær day(t) braa fiskervahtern ee trahktern
Do I need a permit?	**Behöver jag fiskekort?**	berhurverr yaa(g) fiskerkoo^rt

Boats

To explore the archipelagos, the coastline or the inland waterways, you may rent a motorboat or sailing-boat by the week. Or you could hire a rowing-boat or a canoe just for a day.

FOR CAMPING AND COUNTRYSIDE, see page 90

RELAXING

Swimming

You can swim from rocky coves, sandy beaches or grassy banks in Sweden. Thanks to the Gulf Stream the water on the west coast tends to be quite warm. The same can't be said for the sea on the east coast, or the lakes.

Can one swim in the lake/river?	Kan man bada i sjön/floden?	kahn mahn **baa**dah ee shurn/**floo**dern
Is it safe for swimming?	Kan man bada utan risk?	kahn mahn **baa**dah **ew**tahn risk
Is there a lifeguard?	Finns det en livräddare?	finss d$\overline{ay}$(t) ehn **leev**rehdahrer
Is it safe for children?	Är det riskfritt för barn?	ær d$\overline{ay}$(t) **risk**frit furr bah**r**n
There are some big waves.	Det går höga vågor.	d$\overline{ay}$(t) goar **hur**gah **voa**goor
Is it a good place for snorkelling?	Är det en bra plats för att dyka med snorkel?	ær d$\overline{ay}$(t) ehn braa plahtss furr aht **dew**kah mayd **snork**erl
Are there any dangerous currents?	Går det farliga strömmar här?	goar d$\overline{ay}$(t) **faar**liggah **strur**mahr hær
What's the temperature of the water?	Hur många grader är det i vattnet?	h$\overline{ew}$r **mong**ah **graa**derr ær d$\overline{ay}$(t) ee **vaht**nert
I want to hire a/an/some...	Jag skulle vilja hyra...	yaa(g) **skew**ler **vil**yah **hew**rah
air mattress	en luftmadrass	ehn **lewft**mahdrahss
bath towel	ett badlaken	eht **baad**laakahn
bathing hut	en badhytt	ehn **baad**hewt
bathing suit	en baddräkt	ehn **baad**rehkt
deck-chair	en solstol	ehn **sool**stool
skin-diving equipment	en dykar-utrustning	ehn **dew**kahr-**ewt**rewstning
snorkel, goggles and flippers	snorkel, cyklopöga och simfötter	**snork**erl sewkloa**pur**gah ok **sim**furter
sunshade	ett solskydd	eht **sool**shewd
swimming belt	en simdyna	ehn **sim**dewnah
tent	ett tält	eht tehlt
water skis	vattenskidor	**vah**ternsheedoor

Sauna

The Finnish tradition of the sauna bath is extremely popular in Sweden. It combines elements of physical fitness, cleanliness and even a chance for relaxed business talks amid the steam. Then cool off with a shower, a swim, or a roll in the snow!

Winter sports

The climate favours winter sports in Sweden. You can ice-skate on lakes, rivers and even the sea, as well as at artificial skating rinks. Cross-country skiing is particularly popular. Downhill and slalom runs operate in the north far into April. Ski-lifts have also been installed in the vicinity of some larger cities.

What are the skiing conditions like at...?	Hur är skidföret i...?	hewr ær sheedfurrert ee
Are the ski-lifts open now?	Är liftarna öppna nu?	ær liftah^rnah urpnah new
Can I take lessons there?	Kan jag ta skid-lektioner där?	kahn yaa(g) taa sheed-lehkshoonerr dær
Where is there a good place for...?	Var finns det bra terräng för...?	vaar finss day(t) braa tehrehng furr
cross-country skiing	långfärdsåkning	longfæ^rdsoakning
alpine skiing	utförsåkning	ewtfurfsoakning
Where can I hire/buy a/some...?	Var kan jag hyra/ köpa...?	vaar kahn yaa(g) hewrah/khurpah
cross-country skis	ett par löparskidor	eht paar lurpahrsheedoor
ski boots	ett par pjäxor	eht paar pyehksoor
ski poles	ett par stavar	eht paar staavahr
ski wax	skidvalla	sheedvahlah
for dry snow	för torr snö	furr tor snur
for wet snow	för våt snö	furr voat snur
skiing equipment	en skidutrustning	ehn sheedewtrewstning
skiis	ett par skidor	eht paar sheedoor
sled	en kälke	ehn khehlker
Is there a skating-rink near here?	Finns det en skrid-skobana i när-heten?	finss day(t) ehn skri(d)skobaanah ee nærhaytern

Camping—Countryside

There are hundreds of camping sites all over Sweden, usually open from the beginning of June to the end of August. They are classified by one, two or three stars (the latter is the highest rating). You may need an international camping carnet, but you can probably buy it on the spot. If you want to camp on private land, be sure to get permission from the owner first.

Can we camp here?	**Kan vi tälta här?**	kahn vee **tehl**tah hær
Where can one camp for the night?	**Var kan vi tälta över natten?**	vaar kahn vee **tehl**tah **ūr**verr **nah**tern
Is there a camping site near here?	**Finns det någon campingplats i närheten?**	finss dāy(t) **noa**gon **kahm**pingplahtss ee **nær**hāytern
May we camp in your field?	**Skulle vi kunna få tälta på er äng?**	**skew**ler vee **kew**nah foa **tehl**tah poa **āy**r ehng
Can we park our caravan (trailer) here?	**Kan vi ställa vår husvagn här?**	kahn vee **stehl**lah voar **hew**svahngn hær
Is this an official camping site?	**Är det här en auktoriserad campingplats?**	ær dāy(t) hær ehn ahktorri**ssāy**rahd **kahm**pingplahtss
May we light a fire?	**Får vi göra upp eld?**	foar vee **yū**rah ewp ehld
Is drinking water available?	**Finns det dricksvatten?**	finss day(t) **driks**vahtern
Are there shopping facilities on the site?	**Kan vi handla på campingplatsen?**	kahn vee **hahn**dlah poa **kahm**pingplahtsern
Are there...?	**Finns det...?**	finss dāy(t)
baths	**bad**	baad
showers	**duschar**	**dew**shahr
toilets	**toiletter**	tooah**leh**terr

DRICKSVATTEN	FÖRORENAT VATTEN
DRINKING WATER	POLLUTED WATER

What's the charge?	Vad är avgiften?	vaa(d) ær aavyiftern
per day	per dag	pær daag
per person	per person	pær pæ^rsõon
for a car	för en bil	fürr ehn beel
for a tent	för ett tält	fürr eht tehlt
for a caravan (trailer)	för en husvagn	fürr ehn hēwsvahngn
Is there a youth hostel near here?	Finns det något vandrarhem i närheten?	finss dāy(t) noagot vahndrahrhehm ee nærhāytern
Do you know anyone who can put us up for the night?	Känner ni någon som kan ge oss logi i natt?	khehnerr nee noagon som kahn yāy oss loshi ee naht

TÄLTNING FÖRBJUDEN	INGA HUSVAGNAR
NO CAMPING	NO CARAVANS (TRAILERS)

Landmarks

barn	en lada	ehn laadah
boulder	ett stenblock	eht stāynblok
bridge	en bro	ehn brõo
building	en byggnad	eh bewgnahd
canal	en kanal	ehn kahnaal
castle	ett slott	eht slot
chapel	ett kapell	eht kahpehl
church	en kyrka	ehn khewrkah
cliff	en klippa	ehn klippah
crossroads	en vägkorsning	ehn vaigko^rsning
farm	en bondgård	ehn boon(d)goa^rd
ferry	en färja	ehn færyah
field	ett fält	eht fehlt
footpath	en stig	ehn steeg
forest	en skog	ehn skõog
gorge	ett pass	eht pahss
grove	en lund	ehn lewnd
heath	en hed	ehn hāyd
highway	en motorväg	ehn mõotorvaig
hill	en kulle	ehn kewler
house	ett hus	eht hēwss
inn	ett värdshus	eht vær^rdshēwss
lake	en sjö	ehn shür

CAMPING

marsh	ett träsk	eht trehsk
moorland	en hed	ehn hāyd
mountain	ett berg	eht behry
mountain range	en bergskedja	ehn behryskhāydyah
path	en stig	ehn steeg
peak	en topp	ehn top
plantation	en odling	ehn ōōdling
pond	en damm	ehn dahm
pool	en bassäng	ehn bahssaing
railway	ett järnvägsspår	eht yāērnvaigsspoar
ravine	en ravin	ehn rahveen
river	en flod	ehn flōōd
road	en väg	ehn vaig
ruin	en ruin	ehn reween
sea	ett hav	eht haav
spring	en källa	ehn khehlah
stream	en ström	ehn strurm
swamp	en sump	ehn sewmp
tower	ett torn	eht tōōˈn
track	ett spår	eht spoar
tree	ett träd	eht traid
tunnel	en tunnel	ehn tewnerl
valley	en dal	ehn daal
village	en by	ehn bēw
waterfall	ett vattenfall	eht vahternfahl
well	en brunn	ehn brewn
windmill	en väderkvarn	ehn vāēderrkvaaˈn
wood	en skog	ehn skōōg

OBEHÖRIGA ÄGER EJ TILLTRÄDE
NO TRESPASSING

| What's the name of that river? | Vad heter den där floden? | vaa(d) hāyterr dehn dāēr flōōdern |
| How high is that mountain? | Hur högt är det berget? | hewr hurgt āēr dāy(t) behryert |

...and if you're tired of walking, you can always try hitch-hiking—though you may have to wait a long time for a lift.

| Can you give me a lift to...? | Kan jag få följa med till...? | kahn yaa(g) foa furlyah māyd til |

FOR ASKING THE WAY, see also page 144

Making friends

It's easy to start up a conversation with the Swedes, particularly when they learn you're a foreigner. You'll find people hospitable, helpful, and curious about your country.

The formal word for "you" *(ni)*, traditionally the correct form of address between all but close friends and children, is now giving way to the informal *du*. When you are formally introduced, shake hands and say:

How do you do?	**Goddag.***	go**ddaag**
How are you?	**Hur står det till?**	he̅w̅r stoar da̅y̅(t) til
Very well, thank you.	**Tack bra.**	tahk braa
Fine, thanks. And you?	**Fint, tack. Och ni?**	fint tahk. ok nee
May I introduce...	**Får jag presentera...**	foar yaa(g) prehssern-ta̅y̅rah
My name's...	**Mitt namn är...**	mit nahmn a̅e̅r
Glad to know you.	**Trevligt att träffas.**	tra̅y̅vlit aht trehfahss

Follow-up

How long have you been here?	**Hur länge har ni varit här?**	he̅w̅r **lehng**er haar nee vaarit ha̅e̅r
We've been here a week.	**Vi har varit här i en vecka.**	vee haar **vaarit** ha̅e̅r ee ehn **vehkah**
Is this your first visit?	**Är det här ert första besök?**	a̅e̅r da̅y̅(t) ha̅e̅r a̅y̅ʳt fur`ʳ`stah berss**u̅r̅k**
No, we came here last year.	**Nej, vi var här förra året också.**	nay vee vaar ha̅e̅r furrah **oarert** oksoa
Are you enjoying your stay?	**Är ni nöjd med er vistelse?**	a̅e̅r nee nuryd ma̅y̅d a̅y̅r **vis**terlser
Yes, I like...very much.	**Ja, jag tycker mycket om...**	yaa, yaa(g) **tewk**err **mewk**er(t) om

* This is the normal response when introduced to someone.

Are you on your own?	Är ni här ensam?	ǣr nee hǣr ehnsahm
I'm with...	Jag är med...	yaa(g) ǣr māyd
my husband	min man	min mahn
my wife	min fru	min frēw
my family	min familj	min fahmily
my parents	mina föräldrar	meenah furrehldrahr
some friends	några vänner	noagrah vehnerr
Where do you come from?	Varifrån kommer ni?	vaarifroan kommerr nee
I'm from...	Jag kommer från...	yaa(g) kommerr froan
Where are you staying?	Var bor ni?	vaar bōōr nee
I'm a student.	Jag är studerande.	yaa(g) ǣr stewdāyrahn-der
We're here on holiday.	Vi är här på semester.	vee ǣr hǣr poa sehmehsterr
I'm here on business.	Jag är här på affärsresa.	yaa(g) ǣr hǣr poa ahfǣrˢrāyssah
I hope we'll see you again soon.	Jag hoppas vi ses snart igen.	yaa(g) hoppahss vee sāyss snaaʳt iyehn
See you later/See you tomorrow.	Vi ses senare/Vi ses i morgon.	vee sāyss sāynahrer/vee sāyss ee morron

The weather

Always a good topic for conversation, in Sweden as elsewhere.

What a lovely day!	En sån underbar dag!	ehn son ewnderrbaar daa(g)
What awful weather!	Ett sånt förfärligt väder!	eht sont furrfǣrlit vaiderr
Isn't it cold/hot today?	Är det inte kallt/varmt idag?	ǣr dāy(t) inter kahlt/vahrmt iddaa(g)
Do you think it'll... tomorrow?	Tror ni det kommer att...i morgon?	trōōr nee dāy(t) kommerr aht...ee morron
rain/snow	regna/snöa	rehngnah/snʉ̄rah
clear up/be sunny	klarna upp/vara soligt	klaaʳnah ewp/vaarah sōōlit

Invitations

My wife and I would like you to dine with us on...	**Min fru och jag skulle gärna vilja se er på middag hos oss på...**	min frew ok yaa(g) skewler yæᵣnah vilyah say ayr poa middaa(g) hos oss poa
Can you join us for a drink this evening?	**Kan ni komma över på en drink i kväll?**	kahn nee kommah ūrverr poa ehn drink ee kvehl
There's a party. Are you coming?	**Det är ett party. Kommer ni med?**	day(t) ær eht paᵣti. kommerr nee mayd.
That's very kind of you.	**Det var mycket vänligt av er.**	day(t) vaar mewker(t) vehnlit aav ayr
What time shall we come?	**Hur dags skall vi komma?**	hewr dahgss skahl vee kommah
May I bring a friend/girl-friend?	**Får jag ta med en god vän/väninna?**	foar yaa(g) taa mayd ehn good vehn/vehninnah
I'm afraid we've got to go now.	**Tyvärr måste vi nog gå nu.**	tewvær moster vee nōōg goa new
Next time you must come to visit us.	**Nästa gång måste ni komma och hälsa på oss.**	nehstah gong moster nee kommah ok hehlsah poa oss
Thanks for the evening. It was great.	**Tack för i kväll. Det var verkligen kul.**	tahk fūrr ee kvehl. day(t) vaar væᵣkligern kewl

Dating

Would you like a cigarette?	**Får jag bjuda på en cigarrett?**	foar yaa(g) byewdah poa ehn siggahreht
Do you have a light, please?	**Skulle ni kunna ge mig eld?**	skewler nee kewnah yay may ehld
Can I get you a drink?	**Får jag bjuda på en drink?**	foar yaa(g) byewdah poa ehn drink
Excuse me, could you please help me?	**Förlåt mig. Skulle ni kunna hjälpa mig?**	furᵣloat may. skewler nee kewnah yehlpah may
Haven't we met somewhere before?	**Har vi inte träffats förut?**	haar vee inter trehfahts fūrrewt

I'm lost. Can you show me the way to...?	Jag har gått vilse. Kan ni visa mig vägen till...?	yaa(g) haar got vilser. kahn nee veessah may vaigern til
Are you waiting for someone?	Väntar ni på någon?	vehntahr nee poa noagon
Are you free this evening?	Är ni ledig i kväll?	ār nee lāydi(g) ee kvehl
Would you like to go out with me tonight?	Skulle ni vilja gå ut med mig i kväll?	skewler nee vilyah goa ēwt māyd may ee kvehl
Would you like to go dancing?	Skulle ni vilja gå ut och dansa?	skewler nee vilyah goa ēwt ok dahnsah
I know a good discotheque/restaurant.	Jag vet ett bra diskotek/en bra restaurang.	yaa(g) vāyt eht braa diskotāyk/ ehn braa rehstorrahng
Shall we go to the cinema (movies)?	Skall vi gå på bio?	skahl vee goa poa beeo
Would you like to go for a drive?	Har ni lust att ta en biltur?	haar nee lewst aht taa ehn beeltēwr
I'd love to, thank you.	Ja tack, mycket gärna.	yaa tahk mewker(t) yārⁿnah
Where shall we meet?	Var skall vi träffas?	vaar skahl vee trehfahs
I'll call for you at... o'clock.	Jag hämtar er klockan...	yaa(g) hehmtahr āyr klokkahn
May I take you home?	Får jag följa er hem?	foar yaa(g) furlyah āyr hehm
Can I see you again tomorrow?	Får jag träffa er igen i morgon?	foar yaa(g) trehfah āyr iyehn ee morron
Thank you, it's been a wonderful evening.	Tusen tack, det har varit en underbar kväll.	tēwssern tahk dāy(t) haar vaarit ehn ewnderrbaar kvehl
What's your telephone number?	Vad är ert telefonnummer?	vaa(d) ār āyʳt tehlerfoannewmerr
Do you live with your family?	Bor ni med er familj?	bōōr nee māyd āyr fahmily
Do you live alone?	Bor ni ensam?	bōōr nee ehnsahm
What time is your last bus?	Hur dags går er sista buss?	hēwr dahgss goar āyr sistah bewss

Shopping guide

This shopping guide is designed to help find you what you want with ease, accuracy and speed. It features:

1. A list of all major types of shops and services (page 98).
2. Some general expressions needed when shopping to enable you to define your requirements precisely (page 100).
3. Full details of the shops and services likely to concern you; here you'll find advice, phrases, alphabetical lists of items and conversion charts listed under the headings below.

SHOPPING

Shops, stores and services

Most shops are open from 9 or 9.30 to 6 p.m., Monday to
Friday. On Saturdays closing time varies from 1 to 4 p.m.
In larger cities some supermarkets and food sections of
the main department stores may remain open till 8 p.m.
Also in the big cities, small shops selling basic necessities
open on Sundays and till late hours on weekdays.

Where's the nearest...?	Var ligger närmaste...?	vaar liggerr nærmaster
antique shop	antikvitetsaffär	ahntikvit**ay**tsahfær
art gallery	konstgalleri	**konst**gahlerri
bakery	bageri	baagerri
bank	bank	bahnk
barber's	barberare	bahr**bay**rahrer
beautician	skönhetssalong	shurn**hay**tsahlong
beauty salon	damfrisörska	**daam**frissur'skah
bookshop	bokhandel	b**oo**khahnderl
butcher	slaktare	**slah**ktahrer
cable office	telegrafstation	tehler**graaf**stahsh**oo**n
camera shop	fotoaffär	**foo**toahfær
candy store	fruktaffär	**frewkt**ahfær
chemist	apotek	ahpot**ay**k
cigar store	tobaksaffär	t**oo**bahksahfær
cigarette stand	kiosk	**khi**osk
cobbler	skomakare	sk**oo**maakahrer
confectioner	fruktaffär	**frewkt**ahfær
delicatessen	delikatessaffär	dehlikkah**tehss**ahfær
dentist	tandläkare	**tahn**(d)laikahrer
department store	varuhus	**vaa**rewhewss
doctor	doktor	**dok**tor
dressmaker	sömmerska	**surmeh'**skah
drugstore	apotek	ahpot**ay**k
dry-cleaner	kemtvätt	**khaym**tveht
filling station	bensinstation	behn**sseen**stahsh**oo**n
fishmonger	fiskhandlare	**fisk**hahndlahrer
flea market	loppmarknad	**lop**mahrknahd
florist	blomsterhandel	**blom**sterrhahnderl
furrier	körsnär	khur**'snær**
garage	bilverkstad	**beel**værkstaa(d)

greengrocer	grönsaksaffär	grurnsaaksahfær
grocery	speceriaffär	spehsserriahfær
hairdresser (ladies)	damfrisörska	daamfrissur'skah
hardware store	järnhandel	yæ'rnhahnderl
hat shop	modist	moddist
health-food shop	hälsokostbod	hehlsokostbood
hospital	sjukhus	shewkhewss
ironmonger	järnhandel	yæ'rnhahnderl
jeweller	juvelerare	yewverlayrahrer
launderette	snabbtvätt	snahbtveht
laundry	tvättinrättning	tvehtinrehtning
leather-goods store	läderaffär	laiderrahfær
liquor store	systembolag	sewstaymbolaag
market	torg	tory
milliner	modist	moodist
newsagent	pressbyrå	prehsbewroa
news-stand	tidningskiosk	tee(d)ningskhiosk
optician	optiker	optikkerr
pastry shop	finbageri	feenbaagerri
petrol station	bensinstation	behnsseenstahshoon
photo shop	fotoaffär	footoahfær
police station	polisstation	poleesstahshoon
post-office	postkontor	postkontoor
shoemaker (repairs)	skomakare	skoomaakahrer
shoe shop	skoaffär	skooahfær
souvenir shop	souvenirbutik	sooverneerbewteek
sporting-goods shop	sportaffär	spo'tahfær
stationer	pappershandel	pahper'shahnderl
supermarket	snabbköp	snahbkhurp
sweet-shop	fruktaffär	frewktahfær
tailor	skräddare	skrehdahrer
tea shop	konditori	kondittorri
telegraph office	telegraf	tehlergraaf
tobacconist	tobaksaffär	toobahksahfær
toiletry shop	parfymeri	pahrfewmerri
toy-shop	leksaksaffär	layksaaksahfær
travel agent	resebyrå	raysserbewroa
vegetable store	grönsaksaffär	grurnsaaksahfær
veterinarian	veterinär	vehterrinnær
watchmaker	urmakare	ewrmaakahrer
wine merchant	systembolag	sewstaymbolaag

SHOPPING

| **SPECIALERBJUDANDE** | **VRAKPRISER** | **REA** |
| SPECIAL OFFER | BARGAIN | SALES |

General expressions

Here are some expressions which will be useful to you when you're out shopping:

Where?

Where's a good...?	**Var finns ett bra...?**	vaar finss eht braa
Where can I find a...?	**Var finner jag ett...?**	vaar finnerr yaa(g) eht
Where do they sell...?	**Var säljer man...?**	vaar sehlyerr mahn
Can you recommend an inexpensive...?	**Kan ni föreslå en billig...?**	kahn nee fürrersloa ehn billi(g)
Where's the main shopping area?	**Var ligger shoppingcentrum?**	vaar liggerr shopping-sehntrewm
How far is it from here?	**Hur långt är det dit?**	hewr longt ær day(t) deet
How do I get there?	**Hur kommer jag dit?**	hewr kommerr yaa(g) deet

Service

Can you help me?	**Kan ni hjälpa mig?**	kahn nee yehlpah may
I'm just looking around.	**Jag bara ser mig omkring.**	yaa(g) baarah sayr may omkring
I want...	**Jag skulle vilja ha...**	yaa(g) skewler vilyah haa
Can you show me some...?	**Kan ni visa mig några...?**	kahn nee veessah may noagrah
Do you have any...?	**Har ni några...?**	haar nee noagrah

That one

Can you show me...?	**Skulle ni kunna visa mig...?**	skewler nee kewnah veessah may
that/those	**det/de**	day(t)/deh
the one in the window	**det i fönstret**	day(t) ee furnstrert
the one in the display case	**det på hyllan**	day(t) poa hewlahn
It's over there.	**Det är där borta.**	day(t) ær dær bortah

Defining the article

I'd like a...	**Jag skulle vilja ha ett...**	yaa(g) skewler vilyah haa eht
I want a...one	**Jag vill ha något...**	yaa(g) vil haa noagot
big	**stort**	stoo͞rt
coloured	**färgat**	færyaht
dark	**mörkt**	murrkt
good	**gott**	got
light (weight)	**lätt**	leht
light (colour)	**ljust**	yewst
long	**långt**	longt
modern	**modernt**	moodæ͞rnt
natural	**naturligt**	nahte͞wrlit
oval	**ovalt**	oovaalt
rectangular	**rektangulärt**	rehktahngewlæ͞rt
round	**runt**	rewnt
short	**kort**	ko͞rt
small	**litet**	leetert
soft	**mjukt**	myewkt
square	**fyrkantigt**	fe͞wrkahntit
I don't want anything too expensive.	**Det får inte vara för dyrt.**	da͞y(t) foar inter vaarah furr dew͞rt

Preference

Can you show me some more?	**Kan ni visa mig någonting annat?**	kahn nee veessah may noagonting ahnaht
Haven't you anything...?	**Har ni ingenting...**	haar nee ingernting
cheaper/better	**billigare/bättre**	billiggahrer/behtrer
larger/smaller	**större/mindre**	sturrer/mindrer

How much?

How much is it?	**Hur mycket kostar det?**	he͞wr mewker(t) kostahr da͞y(t)
I don't understand.	**Jag förstår inte.**	yaa(g) furrstoar inter
Please write it down.	**Var snäll och skriv ner det.**	vaar snehl ok skreev nayr da͞y(t)
I don't want to spend more than...crowns.	**Jag vill inte lägga ut mer än...kronor.**	yaa(g) vil inter lehgah ewt mayr ehn...kro͞onoor

FOR COLOURS, see page 113

SHOPPING

Decision

It's not quite what I want.	Det är inte riktigt vad jag vill ha.	day(t) ær inter riktit vaa(d) yaa(g) vil haa
No, I don't like it.	Nej, jag tycker inte om det.	nay yaa(g) tewkerr inter om day(t)
I'll take it.	Jag tar det.	yaa(g) taar day(t)

Ordering

| Can you order it for me? | Kan ni beställa det åt mig? | kahn nee berstehlah day(t) oat may |
| How long will it take? | Hur lång tid tar det? | hewr long teed taar day(t) |

Delivery

I'll take it with me.	Jag tar det med mig.	yaa(g) taar day(t) mayd may
Deliver it to the... Hotel.	Var vänlig och leverera det till hotell...	vaar vehnli(g) ok lehverrayrah day(t) til hotehl
Please send it to this address.	Var snäll och sänd det till den här adressen.	vaar snehl ok sehnd day(t) til dehn hær ahdrehssern

Paying

How much is it?	Hur mycket kostar det?	hewr mewker(t) kostahr day(t)
Can I pay by traveller's cheque?	Kan jag betala med resecheck?	kahn yaa(g) bertaalah mayd rayssershehk
Do you accept dollars/pounds/credit cards?	Tar ni emot dollar/pund/kreditkort?	taar nee ehmoot dollahr/pewnd/krehdeetkoo'rt
Haven't you made a mistake in the bill?	Har ni inte gjort ett fel på räkningen?	haar nee inter yoo'rt eht fayl poa raikningern
Can I please have a receipt?	Skulle jag kunna få ett kvitto?	skewler yaa(g) kewnah foa eht kvitto

Anything else?

No, thanks, that's all.	Nej tack, det var allt.	nay tahk day(t) vaar ahlt
Yes, I want...	Ja, jag skulle vilja ha...	yaa, yaa(g) skewler vilyah haa
Show me...	Var snäll och visa mig...	vaar snehl ok veessah may
Thank you. Good-bye.	Tack. Adjö.	tahk. ahyūr

Dissatisfied

Can you please exchange this?	Skulle ni kunna byta det här?	skewler nee kewnah bewtah day(t) hær
I want to return this.	Jag vill lämna tillbaka det här.	yaa(g) vil lehmnah tilbaakah day(t) hær
I'd like a refund. Here's the receipt.	Jag skall be att få pengarna tillbaka. Här är kvittot.	yaa(g) skahl bay aht foa pehngahr'nah tilbaakah hær ær kvittot

SHOPPING

👈	👉
Kan jag hjälpa er?	Can I help you?
Vad önskar ni?	What would you like?
Vilken...önskar ni?	What...would you like?
färg/form kvalitet	colour/shape quality
Tyvärr har vi inga.	I'm sorry, we haven't any.
Det är slut på lagret.	We're out of stock.
Skall vi beställa det åt er?	Shall we order it for you?
Tar ni det med er, eller skall vi skicka det?	Will you take it with you or shall we send it?
Någonting annat?	Anything else?
Det blir...kronor, tack.	That's...crowns, please.
Kassan är därborta.	The cashier's over there.

Bookshop—Stationer's—News-stand

In Sweden, bookshops and stationers are usually separate shops, though the latter often sell paperbacks. Newspapers and magazines are sold at kiosks. Foreign newspapers may be found at most large railway stations.

Where's the nearest...?	**Var ligger närmaste...?**	vaar **ligg**err **nær**mahster
bookshop	**bokhandel**	b̄ookhahnderl
stationer's	**pappershandel**	pahper^rshahnderl
news-stand	**tidningskiosk**	**tee(d)**ningskhiosk
Can you recommend a good bookshop?	**Kan ni rekommendera en bra bokhandel?**	kahn nee rehkommern-**dāȳ**rah ehn braa b̄ookhahnderl
Where can I buy an English newspaper?	**Var kan jag köpa en engelsk tidning?**	vaar kahn yaa(g) **kh̄ur**pah ehn **ehng**erlsk **tee(d)**ning
I want to buy a/an/some...	**Jag skulle vilja köpa...**	yaa(g) **skew**ler **vil**yah **kh̄ur**pah
address book	**en adressbok**	ehn ah**drehs**b̄ook
ball-point pen	**en kulspetspenna**	ehn **kēwl**spehtspehnah
book	**en bok**	ehn b̄ook
box of paints	**en färglåda**	ehn **fær**yloadah
carbon paper	**karbonpapper**	kahr**boan**pahperr
cellophane tape	**en rulle tejp**	ehn **rew**ler tayp
dictionary	**ett lexikon**	eht **lehk**sikkon
Swedish-English	**svensk-engelskt**	svehnsk-**ehng**erlskt
English-Swedish	**engelsk-svenskt**	**ehng**erlsk-svehnskt
pocket dictionary	**ett ficklexikon**	eht **fik**lehksikkon
envelopes	**några kuvert**	**noa**grah kew**vær**
eraser	**ett radergummi**	eht rah**dāȳr**gewmi
file	**en pärm**	ehn pærm
fountain-pen	**en reservoarpenna**	ehn rehssoer**vaar**pehnah
grammar book	**en grammatik**	ehn grahmah**teek**
guide-book	**en guidebok**	ehn **guide**b̄ook
ink	**bläck**	blehk
labels	**etiketter**	ehti**keh**terr
magazine	**en veckotidning**	ehn **veh**kotee(d)ning
map	**en karta**	ehn **kaa**^rtah
map of the town	**stadskarta**	**stahds**kaa^rtah
road map of...	**vägkarta över...**	**vaig**kaa^rtah **ūr**verr

SHOPPING

newspaper	en dagstidning	ehn dahgstee(d)ning
American	amerikansk	ahm(er)rikahnsk
English	engelsk	ehngerlsk
notebook	en anteckningsbok	ehn ahntehkningsbook
paperback	en pocketbok	ehn pokkertbook
paper napkins	pappersservetter	pahper'ssærvehterr
pen	en penna	ehn pehnah
pencil	en blyertspenna	ehn blewer'tspehnah
pencil sharpener	en pennvässare	ehn pehnvehssahrer
playing cards	en kortlek	ehn koo'rtlayk
postcards	några vykort	noagrah vewkoo'rt
refill (for a pen)	en refill	ehn rehfeel
rubber	ett radergummi	eht rahdayrgewmi
ruler	en linjal	ehn linyaal
sketching block	ett skissblock	eht skisblok
string	ett snöre	eht snürrer
tissue paper	lite silkepapper	leeter silkerpahperr
tracing-paper	kalkerpapper	kahlkayrpahperr
typewriter ribbon	ett skrivmaskins-band	eht skreevmahsheens-bahnd
typing-paper	skrivmaskins-papper	skreevmasheens-pahperr
wrapping-paper	omslagspapper	omslaagspahperr
writing-pad	ett skrivblock	eht skreevblok

Where's the guide-book section?
Var är avdelningen för guideböcker?
vaar ær aavdaylningern fürr guideburkerr

Where do you keep the English books?
Var har ni engelska böcker?
vaar haar nee ehngerlskah burkerr

Have you any of...'s books in English?
Har ni några av... s böcker på engelska?
haar nee noagrah aav ...'s burkerr poa ehngerlskah

Is there an English translation of...?
Finns...översatt till engelska?
finss...ürver'saht til ehngerlskah

Camping

Here we're concerned with the equipment you may need.

I'd like a/an/some...	Jag skall be att få...	yaa(g) skahl bay aht foa
axe	en yxa	ehn **ew**ksah
bottle opener	en flasköppnare	ehn **flahsk**urpnahrer
bucket	en hink	ehn hink
butane gas	butangas	bewt**aan**gaas
camp bed	en tältsäng	ehn **tehlt**sehng
camping equipment	en tältutrustning	ehn **tehlt**ewtrewstning
can opener	en konservöppnare	ehn kons**ær**vurpnahrer
candles	stearinljus	stehah**reen**yewss
chair	en stol	ehn stool
folding chair	en fällstol	ehn **fehl**stool
compass	en kompass	ehn kom**pahss**
corkscrew	en korkskruv	ehn **kork**skrewv
crockery	porslin	po**r**sleen
cutlery	bestick	ber**stik**
deck chair	en vilstol	ehn **veel**stool
first-aid kit	en förbandslåda	ehn furr**bahnds**loadah
fishing tackle	fiskedon	fisker**doon**
flashlight	en ficklampa	ehn **fik**lahmpah
frying pan	en stekpanna	ehn **stayk**pahnah
groundsheet	ett tältunderlag	eht **tehl**ew**nder**laag
hammer	en hammare	ehn **hah**mahrer
hammock	en hängmatta	ehn **hehng**mahtah
haversack	en ryggsäck	ehn **rewg**sehk
ice bag	en islåda	ehn **eess**loadah
kerosene	fotogen	fotto**shayn**
kettle	en kittel	ehn **khit**terl
knapsack	en ryggsäck	ehn **rewg**sehk
lamp	en lampa	ehn **lahm**pah
lantern	en lykta	ehn **lewk**tah
matches	tändstickor	**tehn(d)**stikkoor
mattress	en madrass	ehn mah**drahss**
methylated spirits	träsprit	trais**preet**
mosquito net	ett myggnät	eht **mewg**nait
pail	en spann	ehn spahn
paraffin	fotogen	fotto**shayn**
penknife	en pennkniv	ehn **pehn**kneev
picnic case	en picknick-korg	ehn **piknik**-kory
pressure cooker	en tryckkokare	ehn **trewk**kookahrer
primus stove	ett primuskök	eht **pree**mewsk**hurk**
rope	ett rep	eht rayp
rucksack	en ryggsäck	ehn **rewg**sehk

saucepan	en stekpanna	ehn staykpahnah
scissors	en sax	ehn sahks
screwdriver	en korkskruv	ehn korkskrewv
sheathknife	en dolk	ehn dolk
sleeping-bag	en sovsäck	ehn soavsehk
stewpan	en gryta	ehn grewtah
stove	en spis	ehn speess
table	ett bord	eht boo'd
folding-table	ett fällbord	eht fehlboo'd
tent	ett tält	eht tehlt
tent pegs	tältpinnar	tehltpinnahr
tent poles	tältpålar	tehltpoalahr
thermos flask (bottle)	en termosflaska	ehn tærmoosflahskah
tin opener	en konservöppnare	ehn konsærvurpnahrer
tongs	tänger	tehngerr
tool kit	en verktygslåda	ehn værktewgsloadah
torch	en ficklampa	ehn fiklahmpah
wood alcohol	träsprit	traispreet

Crockery

cups	koppar	koppahr
dishes	fat	faat
food-box	matlåda	maatloadah
mugs	muggar	mewgahr
plates	tallrikar	tahlrikkahr
saucers	tefat	tayfaat

Cutlery

forks	gafflar	gahflahr
knives	knivar	kneevahr
spoons	skedar	shaydahr
teaspoons	teskedar	tayshaydahr
(made of) plastic	av plast	aav plahst
(made of)	av rostfritt	aav rostfrit
stainless steel	stål	stoal

Chemist's—Drugstore

Swedish chemists' normally don't stock the great range of goods that you'll find in England or the U.S.A. For example, they don't sell photographic equipment or books. And for perfume, cosmetics etc. you must go to a *parfymeri* (**pahr**fewmerree). Note that you need a prescription for most medicines.

In the window you'll see a notice telling you where the nearest all-night chemist's is.

This section has been divided into two parts:

1. Pharmaceutical—medicine, first-aid etc.
2. Toiletry—toilet articles, cosmetics.

General

Where's the nearest (all-night) chemist's?	**Var ligger närmaste nattapotek?**	vaar liggerr **nær**mahster **naht**ahpotayk
What time does the chemist's open/close?	**Hur dags öppnar/stänger apoteket?**	hewr dahgss **urpnahr/stehng**err ahpo**tayk**ert

Part 1—Pharmaceutical

I want something for...	**Jag skulle vilja ha någonting mot...**	yaa(g) **skew**ler **vil**yah haa **noa**gonting moot
a cold	**en förkylning**	ehn fur**khewl**ning
a cough	**hosta**	**hoo**stah
hay-fever	**hösnuva**	**hür**snewvah
a hangover	**baksmälla**	**baak**smehlah
sunburn	**solsveda**	**sool**svaydah
travel sickness	**ressjuka**	**rays**shewkah
an upset stomach	**dålig mage**	**doa**li(g) **maa**ger
Can you make up this prescription for me?	**Kan jag få ut det här receptet?**	kahn yaa(g) foa ewt day(t) hær reh**ssehp**tert
Can I get it without a prescription?	**Kan jag få det utan recept?**	kahn yaa(g) foa day(t) **ew**tahn reh**ssehpt**

FOR DOCTOR, see page 162

Can I have a/an/some...?	Skulle jag kunna få...?	skewler yaa(g) kewnah foa
ammonia	lite ammoniak	leeter ahmooniahk
antiseptic cream	en antiseptisk kräm	ehn ahntissehptisk kraim
bandage	ett bandage	eht bahndaash
calcium tablets	kalktabletter	kahlktahblehterr
chlorine tablets	klortabletter	kloartahblehterr
contraceptives	preventivmedel	prehvernteevmayderl
corn-plasters	liktornsplåster	leektoornsplosterr
cotton wool	ett paket bomull	eht pahkayt boomewl
cough-drops	hostmedecin	hoostmehdersseen
diabetic lozenges	insulintabletter	insewleentahblehterr
disinfectant	desinficerings-medel	dehssinfissayrings-mayderl
ear-drops	örondroppar	urrondroppahr
eye-drops	ögondroppar	urgondroppahr
first-aid kit	förbandslåda	furrbahndsloadah
gargle	gurgelvatten	gewrgerlvahtern
gauze	några kompresser	noagrah komprehsserr
insect repellent	insektsdödare	insehktsdurdahrer
iodine	jod	yod
iron-pills	järntabletter	yærntahblehterr
laxative	laxermedel	lahksayrmayderl
lint	bomullsbandage	boomewlsbahndaash
mouthwash	munvatten	mewnvahtern
painkiller	tabletter mot värk	tahblehterr moot værk
plaster	plåster	plosterr
quinine tablets	kinintabletter	kinnintahblehterr
sanitary napkins	dambindor	daambindoor
sedative	lugnande medel	lewngnahnder mayderl
sleeping-pills	sömntabletter	surmntahblehterr
stomach pills	magpiller	maagpillerr
thermometer	termometer	tehrmoomayterr
throat lozenges	halspastiller	hahlspahstillerr
tissues	ansiktsservetter	ahnsiktssævehterr
tonic	ansiktsvatten	ahnsiktssvahtern
tranquillizers	lugnande medel	lewngnahnder mayderl
vitamin pills	vitamintabletter	vittahmeentahblehterr

SHOPPING

GIFT!	POISON!
ENDAST FÖR UTVÄRTES BRUK!	FOR EXTERNAL USE ONLY

Part 2—Toiletry

SHOPPING

I'd like a/an/ some...	Jag skulle vilja ha...	yaa(g) skewler vilyah haa
acne cream	en salva mot finnar	ehn sahlvah moot finnahr
after-shave lotion	rakvatten	raakvahtern
astringent	sammandragande medel	sahmahndraagahnder mayderl
bath essence	badolja	baadolyah
bath salts	badsalt	baadsahlt
cologne	eau de cologne	oa deh collong
cream	en kräm	ehn kraim
cleansing cream	rengöringskräm	raynyurringskraim
cuticle cream	nagelbandskräm	naagerlbahndskraim
foundation cream	puderunderlag	pewderrewnderrlaag
moisturizing cream	fuktighets- bevarande kräm	fewktighayts- bervaarahnder kraim
night cream	nattkräm	nahtkraim
cuticle remover	nagelbandsvatten	naagerlbahndsvahtern
emery board	sandpappersfilar	sahndpahper'sfeelahr
eye liner	en eye liner	ehn eye liner
eye pencil	en ögonpenna	ehn urgonpehnah
eye shadow	ögonskugga	urgonskewgah
face flannel	en tvättlapp	ehn tvehtlahp
face pack	en ansiktsmask	ehn ahnsiktsmahsk
face powder	ansiktspuder	ahnsiktspewderr
foot cream	fotkräm	footkraim
hand cream/lotion	handkräm	hahn(d)kraim
lipsalve	cerat	særaat
lipstick	ett läppstift	eht lehpstift
lipstick brush	en läppstiftspensel	ehn lehpstiftspehnserl
make-up bag	en sminkväska	ehn sminkvehskah
make-up remover pads	avsminknings- servetter	aavsminknings- særvehterr
mascara	ögontusch	urgontewsh
nail brush	en nagelborste	ehn naagerlbo'ster
nail clippers	en nagelklippare	ehn naagerlklippahrer
nail file	en nagelfil	ehn naagerlfeel
nail polish	en nagellack	ehn naagerllahk
nail polish remover	lackborttagnings- medel	lahkbo'taagnings- mayderl
nail scissors	en nagelsax	ehn naagerlsahks
nail strengthener	stärkande medel för naglarna	stærkahnder mayderl furr naaglah'nah
paper handkerchiefs	pappersnäsdukar	pahper'snaisdewkahr

perfume	en parfym	ehn pahr<u>fewm</u>
powder puff	en pudervippa	ehn <u>pew</u>derrvippah
rouge	rouge	r<u>oo</u>sh
safety-pins	säkerhetsnålar	saikerr<u>hay</u>tsnoalahr
shaving brush	en rakborste	ehn raakbo^rster
shaving cream	rakkräm	raakraim
shaving soap	en raktvål	ehn raaktvoal
soap	en tvål	ehn tvoal
sun-tan cream/oil	solkräm/sololja	s<u>oo</u>lkraim/s<u>oo</u>lolyah
talcum powder	talk	tahlk
toilet paper	toalettpapper	tooah<u>leht</u>pahperr
toilet water	eau de toilette	oa deh tooah<u>leht</u>
toothbrush	en tandborste	ehn <u>tahn(d)</u>bo^rster
toothpaste	tandkräm	<u>tahn(d)</u>kra<u>im</u>
towel	en handduk	ehn <u>hahn</u>dewk
tweezers	en pincett	en pin<u>seht</u>
washcloth	en tvättlapp	ehn <u>tveht</u>lahp

For your hair

bobby-pins	några hårspännen	noagrah <u>hoar</u>spehnern
comb	en kam	ehn kahm
curlers	några papiljotter	noa<u>grah</u> pahpil<u>yo</u>tterr
dye/tint	ett toningsmedel	eht <u>too</u>ningsmayderl
grips	hårklämmor	<u>hoar</u>klehmoor
hairbrush	en hårborste	ehn hoarbo^rster
hair colouring	hårfärgnings-medel	hoar<u>fær</u>ynings-mayderl
hairnet	ett hårnät	eht hoa^rnait
hair oil	hårolja	<u>hoar</u>olyah
hairpins	hårnålar	hoa^rnoalahr
hair spray	hårspray	hoa^rspray
rollers	rullar	<u>rew</u>lahr
setting lotion	läggningsvätska	<u>lehg</u>ningsvehtskah

For the baby

baby cream	en barnsalva	ehn baa^rnsahlvah
baby food	barnmat	baa^rnmaat
baby powder	baby-puder	baibi-<u>pew</u>derr
bib	en nappflaska	ehn <u>nahp</u>flahskah
dummy (pacifier)	en napp	ehn nahp
nappies (diapers)	blöjor	<u>blury</u>oor
plastic pants	blöjbyxor	<u>blury</u>bewksoor

Clothing

If you want to buy something specific, prepare yourself in advance. Look at the list of clothing on page 117. Get some idea of the colour, material and size you want. They're all listed on the next few pages.

General

I'd like...	**Jag skulle vilja ha...**	yaa(g) **skew**ler **vil**yah haa
I want...for a 10-year-old boy.	**Jag skulle vilja ha...för en 10-årig pojke.**	yaa(g) **skew**ler **vil**yah haa...furr ehn 10-oari(g) **poy**ker
I want something like this.	**Jag skulle vilja ha någonting liknande.**	yaa(g) **skew**ler **vil**yah haa **noa**gonting **leek**nahnder
How much is that per metre?	**Hur mycket kostar det per meter?**	hewr **mew**ker(t) **kost**ahr day(t) pær **may**terr

1 centimetre =	0.39 in.	1 inch = 2.54 cm.
1 metre =	39.37 in.	1 foot = 30.5 cm.
10 metres =	32.81 ft.	1 yard = 0.91 m.

Colour

I want something in...	**Jag skulle vilja ha någonting i...**	yaa(g) **skew**ler **vil**yah haa **noa**gonting ee
I want something to match this.	**Jag skulle vilja ha någonting som passar till det här.**	yaa(g) **skew**ler **vil**yah haa **noa**gonting som **pahss**ahr till day(t) hær
I don't like the colour.	**Jag tycker inte om färgen.**	yaa(g) **tew**kerr inter om **fær**yern

randigt
(rahndit)

prickigt
(prikkit)

rutigt
(rewtit)

mönstrat
(murnstraht)

beige	**beige**	baish
black	**svart**	svah^rt
blue	**blå**	bloa
brown	**brun**	brewn
cream	**krämfärgad**	kraimfæryahd
crimson	**knallröd**	knahlrurd
emerald	**smaragdgrön**	smahrahgdgrurn
fawn	**gulbrun**	gewlbrewn
gold	**guldfärgad**	gewldfæryahd
green	**grön**	grurn
grey	**grå**	groa
mauve	**lila**	leelah
orange	**brandgul**	brahngewl
pink	**rosa**	roassah
purple	**violett**	veeooleht
red	**röd**	rurd
scarlet	**scharlakansröd**	shahlaakahnsrurd
silver	**silverfärgad**	silverrfæryahd
tan	**ljusbrun**	yewssbrewn
turquoise	**turkosblå**	tewrkoosbloa
white	**vit**	veet
yellow	**gul**	gewl

Material

Do you have anything in...?	**Har ni någonting i...?**	haar nee **noa**gonting ee
Is it...?	**Är den...?**	ær dehn
a permanent crease	**permanent- pressad**	pehrmah**neh**nt- prehssahd
hand-made	**handgjord**	hahn(d)yoo^rd
imported	**importerad**	impo^rtayrahd
made here	**tillverkad här**	tillværkahd hær
synthetic	**syntetisk**	sewn**tay**tisk
tapered	**figursydd**	fig**ew**^rsewd
wash-and-wear	**strykfri**	st**rew**kfree
wrinkle-free	**skrynkelfri**	skrewnkerlfree
I want something...	**Jag skulle vilja ha någonting...**	yaa(g) **skew**ler **vil**yah haa **noa**gonting
lighter/heavier	**lättare/tyngre**	**leh**tahrer/**tewng**rer
Do you have any better quality?	**Har ni en bättre kvalitet?**	haar nee ehn **beh**trer kvahli**tay**t

What's it made of?	Vad är det av?	vaa(d) ǣr dāȳ aav
It may be made of...	Det är av...	dāȳ(t)n ǣr aav
camel-hair	kamelhår	kahmāylhoar
chiffon	chiffong	shiffong
corduroy	manchester-sammet	mahnkhesterr-sahmert
cotton	bomull	boomewl
crêpe	crêpe	krehp
denim	jeanstyg	yeenstewg
felt	filt	filt
flannel	flanell	flahnehl
gabardine	gabardin	gahbah'deen
lace	spets	spehtss
leather	läder	laiderr
linen	linne	linner
nylon	nylon	newloan
pique	piké	pikkay
poplin	poplin	popleen
satin	satäng	sahtehng
seersucker	bäck-och-bölja	behk-ok-burlyah
serge	cheviot, sars	shayviot, saa'ss
silk	silke, siden	silker, seedern
suède	mocka	mokkah
taffeta	taft	tahft
terrycloth	frotté	frottay
towelling	handduksväv	hahndewksvaiv
tulle	tyll	tewl
tweed	tweed	tveed
velvet	sammet	sahmert
velour	velour, plysch	verloor, plewsh
wool	ylle	ewler
worsted	kamgarn	kahmgaarn

Size

I take size 38.	Jag har storlek 38.	yaa(g) haar stoo'layk 38
Could you measure me?	Skulle ni kunna ta mina mått?	skewler nee kewnah taa meenah mot
I don't know the Swedish sizes.	Jag känner inte till de svenska storlekarna.	yaa(g) khehnerr inter til deh svehnskah stoo'laykah'nah

For sizes, look at the charts on the next page.

This is your size

Ladies

Dresses/Suits						
American	10	12	14	16	18	20
British	32	34	36	38	40	42
Continental	38	40	42	44	46	48

Stockings							Shoes			
American } British }	8	8½	9	9½	10	10½	6 4½	7 5½	8 6½	9 7½
Continental	0	1	2	3	4	5	37	38	40	41

Gentlemen

Suits/Overcoats							Shirts			
American } British }	36	38	40	42	44	46	15	16	17	18
Continental	46	48	50	52	54	56	38	41	43	45

Shoes									
American } British }	5	6	7	8	8½	9	9½	10	11
Continental	38	39	41	42	43	43	44	44	45

In Europe sizes vary somewhat from country to country, so the above must be taken as an approximate guide.

A good fit?

Can I try it on?	**Kan jag få prova den?**	kahn yaa(g) foa **proo**vah dehn
Where's the fitting room?	**Var är provrummet?**	vaar ær **proo**vrewmert
Does it fit?	**Passar den?**	**pah**ssahr dehn
How long will it take to alter?	**Hur lång tid tar det att ändra den?**	hewr long teed taar day(t) aht **ehn**drah dehn

FOR NUMBERS, see page 175

Shoes

I'd like a pair of...	**Jag skulle vilja ha ett par...**	yaa(g) **skewler** vilyah haa eht paar
shoes/sandals boots/slippers	**skor/sandaler stövlar/tofflor**	skoor/sahndaalerr sturvlahr/tofloor
These are too...	**Dessa är för...**	dehssah ær furr
narrow/wide large/small	**trånga/vida stora/små**	trongah/veedah stoorah/smoa
They pinch my toes.	**De tar i tårna.**	deh taar ee toarnah
Do you have a larger size?	**Har ni ett större nummer?**	haar nee eht **sturrer** newmerr
I want a smaller size.	**Jag skulle vilja ha en mindre storlek.**	yaa(g) **skewler** vilyah haa ehn mindrer stoorlayk
Do you have the same in...?	**Har ni samma i...?**	haar nee sahmah ee
brown/beige black/white	**brunt/beige svart/vitt**	brewnt/baish svahrt/vit
I'd like some shoe polish/shoe laces.	**Jag skulle vilja ha lite skosmörja/ några skosnören.**	yaa(g) **skewler** vilyah haa leeter skoosmurryah/noagrah skoosnurrern

Shoes worn out? Here's the key to getting them repaired:

Can you repair these shoes?	**Kan ni laga de här skorna?**	kahn nee **laa**gah deh hær skoornah
I want new soles and heels.	**Jag skulle vilja ha nya sulor och klackar.**	yaa(g) **skewler** vilyah haa **newah sewl**oor ok klahkahr
When will they be ready?	**När blir de klara?**	nær bleer deh **klaa**rah
I'd like a shine.	**Jag skulle gärna vilja ha dem putsade.**	yaa(g) **skewler** yærnah vilyah haa dehm **pewt**sahder

Clothes and accessories

I'd like a/an/some...	Jag skulle vilja ha...	yaa(g) skewler vilyah haa
anorak	en anorak	ehn ahnorahk
bathing cap	en badmössa	ehn baadmurssah
bathing suit	en baddräkt	ehn baadrehkt
bath robe	en badkappa	ehn baadkahpah
blazer	en blazer	ehn blaisserr
blouse	en blus	ehn blewss
bow tie	en fluga	ehn flewgah
bra	en behå	ehn bayhoa
braces	ett par hängslen	eht paar hehngslehn
briefs	ett par kalsonger	eht paar kahlsongerr
cap	en mössa	ehn murssah
cardigan	en kofta	ehn koftah
coat	en kappa	ehn kahpah
costume	en dräkt	ehn drehkt
dress	en klänning	ehn klehning
dressing gown	en morgonrock	ehn morronrok
evening dress (ladies)	en aftonklänning	ehn ahftonklehning
fur coat	en päls	ehn pehlss
galoshes	ett par galoscher	eht paar gahlosherr
garter belt	en strumphållare	ehn strewmphollahrer
girdle	en höfthållare	ehn hurfthollahrer
gloves	ett par handskar	eht paar hahn(d)skahr
handkerchief	en näsduk	ehn naisdewk
hat	en hatt	ehn haht
headscarf	en scarf	ehn skaaf
jeans	ett par jeans	eht paar jeenss
jumper (Br.)	en jumper	ehn yewmperr
jumper (Am.)	ett förkläde	eht furrkleh(der)
nightdress	ett nattlinne	eht nahtlinner
overcoat	en överrock	ehn ūrverrok
panties	ett par trosor	eht paar trōossoor
pants suit	en byxdräkt	ehn bewksdrehkt
panty girdle	en byxgördel	ehn bewksyūrʳderl
panty hose	ett par strump-byxor	eht paar strewmp-bewksoor
petticoat	en underkjol	ehn ewnderrkhōol
pinafore	ett förkläde	eht furrkleh(der)
pullover	en jumper	ehn yewmperr
pyjamas	en pyjamas	ehn pewyaamahss
raincoat	en regnkappa	ehn rehngnkahpah
robe	en morgonrock	ehn morronrok
rubber boots	gummistövlar	gewmisturvlahr

118

sandals	**sandaler**	sahn**daal**err
shirt	**en skjorta**	ehn **shoo**rtah
shoes	**ett par skor**	eht paar skoor
shorts	**ett par shorts**	eht paar sho**r**tss
skirt	**en kjol**	ehn khool
slip	**en underkjol**	ehn **ewn**derrkhool
slippers	**ett par tofflor**	eht paar **tof**loor
socks	**ett par sockor**	eht paar **sok**koor
sports jacket	**en sportjacka**	ehn spo**r**tyahkah
stockings	**ett par strumpor**	eht paar **strew**mpoor
stole	**en stola**	ehn stoolah
suit (men's)	**en kostym**	ehn kos**tew**m
suit (ladies')	**en dräkt**	ehn drehkt
suspender belt	**en strumphållare**	ehn **strew**mphollahrer
suspenders	**ett par hängslen**	eht paar **hehng**slern
sweater	**en tröja**	ehn **tru**ryah
tennis shoes	**ett par tennisskor**	eht paar **teh**niskoor
tie	**en slips**	ehn slips
tights	**ett par strump-byxor**	eht paar **strew**mp-bewksoor
towel	**handduk**	ehn **hahn**dewk
track suit	**en träningsoverall**	ehn **trai**ningsovverrahl
trousers	**ett par långbyxor**	eht paar **long**bewksoor
twin-set	**ett jumperset**	eht **yewm**perrseht
umbrella	**ett paraply**	eht pahrah**plew**
underpants (men's)	**ett par kalsonger**	eht paar kahl**song**err
undershirt	**en undertröja**	ehn **ewn**derrtruryah
vest (Am.)	**en väst**	ehn vehst
vest (Br.)	**en undertröja**	ehn **ewn**derrtruryah
waistcoat	**en väst**	ehn vehst

belt	**ett skärp**	eht shairp
buckle	**ett spänne**	eht **speh**ner
button	**en knapp**	ehn knahp
collar	**en krage**	ehn **kraa**ger
cuffs	**manschetter**	mahn**sheh**terr
elastic	**ett resårband**	eht reh**ssoar**bahnd
hem	**en fåll**	ehn fol
lapel	**ett rockuppslag**	eht **rokk**ewpslaag
lining	**ett foder**	eht fooderr
pocket	**en ficka**	ehn **fik**kah
ribbon	**ett band**	eht bahnd
sleeve	**en ärm**	ehn ærm
zip (zipper)	**ett blixtlås**	eht **blikst**loass

Electrical appliances and accessories—Records

Beware of the complications of Swedish electricity: Depending on where you are, the current may be 127 or 220 volts, 50 cycles. British and American plugs don't fit Swedish sockets.

What's the voltage?	**Vad är det för strömstyrka?**	vaa(d) ær dāy(t) fūrr strurmstewrkah
I want a plug for this.	**Jag skulle vilja ha en stickkontakt för det här.**	yaa(g) skewler vilyah haa ehn stikkontahkt fūrr dāy(t) hær
Do you have a battery for this...?	**Har ni ett batteri till det här...?**	haar nee eht bahterri til dāy(t) hær
This is broken. Can you repair it?	**Det här är sönder. Kan ni laga det?**	dāy(t) hær ær surnderr. kahn nee laagah dāy(t)
When will it be ready?	**När blir det klart?**	nær bleer dāy(t) klaaʳt
I'd like a/an/some...	**Jag skulle vilja ha...**	yaa(g) skewler vilyah haa
adaptor	**adapter**	ahdahpterr
amplifier	**en förstärkare**	ehn furˈstærkahrer
battery	**ett batteri**	eht bahterri
blender	**en köksassistent**	ehn kurksassistehnt
calculator	**fickräknare**	fikraiknahrer
clock	**en klocka**	ehn klokkah
wall clock	**en väggklocka**	ehn vehgklokkah
food mixer	**en elektrisk visp**	ehn ehlehktrisk visp
hair dryer	**en hårtork**	ehn hoaʳtork
iron	**ett strykjärn**	eht strēwkyæʳn
travelling-iron	**ett resestrykjärn**	eht rāysserstrēwkyæʳn
kettle	**en kastrull**	ehn kahstrewl
percolator	**en kaffebryggare**	ehn kahferbrewgahrer
plug	**en stickkontakt**	ehn stikkontahkt
radio	**en radio**	ehn raadio
car radio	**en bilradio**	ehn beelraadio
portable radio	**en transistor**	ehn trahnsistor
razor	**en rakapparat**	ehn raakahpahraat
record player	**en grammofon**	ehn grahmoffoan
portable record player	**en resegrammofon**	ehn rāyssergrahmoffoan
speakers	**högtalare**	hūrgtaalahrer

SHOPPING

tape recorder	en bandspelare	ehn **bahnd**spāylahrer
cassette tape recorder	en kassettband-spelare	ehn kah**sseht**bahnd-spāylahrer
portable tape recorder	en reseband-spelare	ehn **rāy**sserbahnd-spāylahrer
television	en TV	ehn **tāy**vay
colour television	en färg-TV	ehn **færy**-tāyvay
portable television	en transportabel TV	ehn trahnspo**r**taaberl **tāy**vay
toaster	en brödrost	ehn br**ū**drost
transformer	en transformator	ehn trahnsfor**maa**toor

Record shop

Do you have any records by...?	Har ni några skivor av...?	haar nee **noa**grah **sheev**oor aav
Can I listen to this record?	Kan jag lyssna på den här skivan?	kahn yaa(g) **lews**nah poa dehn hær **sheev**ahn
I'd like a cassette/cartridge.	Jag skulle vilja ha en kassett/en kassett med åtta spår.	yaa(g) **skew**ler **vily**ah haa ehn kah**sseht**/ehn kah**sseht** māyd ottah spoar

| 33/45 rpm | 33/45 varvs | trehti**trāy**/fur**r**ti**fehm** vahrvss |
| mono/stereo | mono/stereo | mono/stereo |

chamber music	kammarmusik	**kah**mahrmewsseek
classical music	klassisk musik	**klah**ssisk mewsseek
folk music	folkmusik	**folk**mewsseek
instrumental music	instrumental-musik	instrewmehn**taal**-mewsseek
jazz	jazz	yass
light music	lätt musik	leht mewsseek
orchestral music	orkestermusik	or**kehs**terrmewsseek
pop music	pop	pop

Hairdressing

Barber's

I'm in a hurry.	**Jag har bråttom.**	yaa(g) haar brottom
I want a haircut, please.	**Jag skulle vilja ha håret klippt.**	yaa(g) skewler vilyah haa hoarert klipt
I'd like a shave.	**Jag skulle vilja bli rakad.**	yaa(g) skewler vilyah blee raakahd
Don't cut it too short.	**Klipp det inte för kort.**	klip dāy(t) inter fūrr koᵉt
Scissors only, please.	**Endast med sax, tack.**	ehndahst māyd sahks tahk
A razor cut, please.	**Var snäll och skär det med rakblad.**	vaar snehl ok shǣr dāy(t) māyd raakblaad
Don't use the clippers.	**Var snäll och använd inte klippnings- maskinen.**	vaar snehl ok ahnvehnd inter klipningsmahsheenern
Just a trim, please.	**Putsa bara lite, tack.**	pewtsah baarah leeter tahk
That's enough off.	**Tack, det räcker.**	tahk dāy(t) rehkerr
A little more off the...	**Lite mer...**	leeter māyr
back	**där bak**	dǣr baak
neck	**i nacken**	ee nahkern
sides	**på sidorna**	poa seedoᵉnah
top	**på hjässan**	poa yehssahn
Please don't use any oil/cream.	**Var vänlig och använd ingen olja/kräm.**	vaar vehnli(g) ok ahnvehnd ingern olyah/kraim
Would you please trim my...?	**Skulle ni kunna putsa...?**	skewler nee kewnah pewtsah
beard	**skägget**	skehgert
moustache	**mustachen**	mewstaashern
sideboards (sideburns)	**polisongerna**	polissongeᵉnah
Thank you. That's fine.	**Tack, det är bra.**	tahk dāy(t) ǣr braa
How much do I owe you?	**Hur mycket blir jag skyldig?**	hēwr mewker(t) bleer yaa(g) shewldi(g)

SHOPPING

FOR TIPPING, see inside back-cover

Ladies' hairdresser's—Beauty salon

Can I make an appointment for sometime on...?	**Skulle jag kunna beställa tid för...?**	skewler yaa(g) kewnah berstehlah teed fürr
I'd like it cut and shaped.	**Jag skall be att få det klippt och lagt.**	yaa(g) skahl bay aht foa day(t) klipt ok lahgt

with a fringe (bangs)	**med lugg**	mayd lewg
page-boy style	**i page**	ee paash
a razor cut	**skuret med rakblad**	skewrert mayd raakblaad
a re-style	**en ny frisyr**	ehn new frissewr
with ringlets	**med lockar**	mayd lokkahr
with waves	**med vågor**	mayd voagoor
in a bun	**i knut**	ee knewt

I want a...	**Jag skulle vilja ha en...**	yaa(g) skewler vilyah haa ehn
bleach	**blekning**	blaykning
colour rinse	**färgsköljning**	færyshurlyning
dye	**färgning**	færyning
permanent wave	**permanent**	pehrmahnehnt
shampoo and set/ blow dry	**tvättning och läggning/föning**	tvehtning ok lehgning/furning
tint	**toning**	tooning
touch-up	**kamning**	kahmning
I want...	**Jag skulle vilja ha...**	yaa(g) skewler vilyah haa
the same colour	**samma färg**	sahmah færy
a darker colour	**en mörkare färg**	ehn murrkahrer færy
a lighter colour	**en ljusare färg**	ehn yewssahrer færy
auburn/blond/ brunette	**kastanjefärgat/ blont/brunt**	kahstahnyerfæryaht/ blont/brewnt
manicure/pedicure/ a face-pack	**manikyr/pedikyr/ ansiktsmask**	mahnikkewr/ pehdikkewr/ ahnsiktsmahsk
I don't want any hairspray.	**Jag vill inte ha någon spray, tack.**	yaa(g) vil inter haa noagon spray tahk

Jeweller's—Watchmaker's

Swedish craftsmen work in all kinds of materials, such as gold, platinum, copper, pewter and steel, but the favourite metal of artists and craftsmen alike is silver. You will find outstanding pieces of jewellery and applied art in traditional as well as modern style.

Can you repair this watch?	**Skulle ni kunna laga den här klockan?**	skewler nee kewnah laagah dehn här klokkahn
Can you change the battery?	**Kan ni byta batteriet?**	kahn nee bewtah bahterriert
The...is broken.	**...är sönder.**	...ær surnderr
glass/spring strap/winder	**glaset/fjädern remmen/upp-dragsverket**	glaassert/fyaiderᶠn rehmern/ewp-draagsvehrkert
When will it be ready?	**När blir den klar?**	nær bleer dehn klaar
I'm just looking around.	**Jag bara ser mig omkring.**	yaa(g) baarah sāyr may omkring
I'd like a cheap watch.	**Jag skulle vilja ha en billig klocka.**	yaa(g) skewler vilyah haa ehn billi(g) klokkah
I want a small gift.	**Jag skulle vilja köpa en liten present.**	yaa(g) skewler vilyah khūrpah ehn leetern prehssehnt
I don't want anything too expensive.	**Jag vill inte ha någonting för dyrt.**	yaa(g) vil inter haa noagonting fūrr dewᶠt
I want something...	**Jag skulle vilja ha något...**	yaa(g) skewler vilyah haa noagot
better/cheaper	**bättre/billigare**	behtrer/billiggahrer
Do you have anything in gold?	**Har ni någonting i guld?**	haar nee noagonting ee gewld
Is this real silver?	**Är detta rent silver?**	ær dehtah rāynt silverr
Can you engrave my initials on it?	**Skulle ni kunna gravera in mina initialer?**	skewler nee kewnah grahvāyrah in meenah innissiaalerr

When you go to a jeweller's, you've probably got some idea of what you want beforehand. Using the following lists (which also include some fancy goods), find out what the article is called and what it's made of.

What is it?

I'd like a/an/some...	Jag skulle vilja ha...	yaa(g) skewler vilyah haa
ashtray	en askkopp	ehn ahskop
beads	ett pärlhalsband	eht pä^rlhahlsbahnd
bracelet	ett armband	eht ahrmbahnd
charm bracelet	med berlocker	mayd berrlokkerr
brooch	en brosch	ehn broash
chain	en kedja	ehn khaydyah
charm	en berlock	ehn berrlok
cigarette case	ett cigarrettetui	eht siggahrehtehtewi
cigarette lighter	en cigarrettändare	ehn siggahrehttehndahrer
clip	ett klips	eht klips
clock	en klocka	ehn klokkah
alarm clock	en väckarklocka	ehn vehkahrklokkah
travelling-clock	ett reseur	eht raysserewr
cross	ett kors	eht ko^rss
cuff links	ett par manschett- knappar	eht paar mahnsheht- knahpahr
cutlery	bestick	berstik
earrings	ett par örhängen	eht paar ūrrhehngern
handbag	en handväska	ehn hahn(d)vehskah
jewel box	ett juvelskrin	eht yewvaylskreen
knife	en kniv	ehn kneev
manicure set	ett manikyrset	eht mahnikewrseht
mechanical pencil	en stiftpenna	ehn stiftpehnah
necklace	ett halsband	eht hahlsbahnd
pendant	ett hängsmycke	eht hehngsmewker
pin	en nål	ehn noal
powder compact	en puderdosa	ehn pewderrdoossah
propelling pencil	en stiftpenna	ehn stiftpehnah
purse	en portmonnä	ehn po^rtmonnay
ring	en ring	ehn ring
silverware	ett silverföremål	eht silverrfurrermoal
statuette	en statyett	ehn stahteweht
strap	en rem	ehn rehm
tie clip	en slipsklämma	ehn slipsklehmah
tie pin	en kråsnål	ehn kroasnoal

wallet	en plånbok	ehn **ploan**book
watch	en klocka	ehn **klok**kah
calendar watch	**med datum-visare**	mayd **daa**tewm-veessahrer
quartz watch	**quartzur**	**kvah't**chewr
wristwatch	**en armbands-klocka**	ehn **ahrm**bahnds-klokkah
shock-resistant	**stötsäker**	**sturt**saikerr
waterproof	**vattentät**	**vah**terntait
with a seconds hand	**med sekund-visare**	mayd ser**kewnd**-veessahrer
watch band	**ett klockarmband**	eht **klok**kahrmbahnd

What's it made of?

alabaster	**alabaster**	ahlah**bah**sterr
amber	**bärnsten**	bæ**r**nstayn
amethyst	**ametist**	ahmer**tist**
brass	**mässing**	**meh**ssing
bronze	**brons**	bronss
copper	**koppar**	**kop**pahr
crystal	**kristall**	kris**tahl**
cut glass	**slipat glas**	**slee**paht glaass
diamond	**diamant**	diah**mahnt**
ebony	**ebenholts**	**eh**bernholtss
emerald	**smaragd**	smah**rahgd**
enamel	**emalj**	eh**mah**ly
glass	**glas**	glaass
gold	**guld**	gewld
gold plate	**gulddoublé**	gewld**dob**lay
ivory	**elfenben**	**ehl**fernbayn
jade	**jade**	yaadh
leather	**läder**	**lai**derr
marble	**marmor**	**mahr**moor
onyx	**onyx**	**oo**newks
pearl	**pärlemor**	**pæ**rlermoor
pewter	**tenn**	tehn
platinum	**platina**	**plaa**tinnah
ruby	**rubin**	rew**been**
sapphire	**safir**	sah**feer**
silver	**silver**	**sil**verr
silver plate	**nysilver**	**new**silverr
stainless steel	**rostfritt stål**	**rost**frit stoal
topaz	**topas**	to**paass**
turquoise	**turkos**	tewr**kooss**

SHOPPING

Laundry—Dry-cleaning

Where's the nearest laundry/dry-cleaner's?	Var ligger närmaste tvättinrättning/kemtvätt?	vaar liggerr **nær**mahster **tveht**inrehtning/**khāȳm**tveht
I want these clothes...	Jag skall be att få de här kläderna...	yaa(g) skahl bāȳ aht foa deh hær **klaider**nah
cleaned	kemtvättade	**khāȳm**tvehtahder
ironed	strukna	**strēw**knah
pressed	pressade	**prehss**ahder
washed	tvättade	**tveht**ahder
When will they be ready?	När blir de klara?	nær bleer deh **klaar**ah
I need them...	Jag behöver dem...	yaa(g) ber**hūr**verr dehm
today	idag	**iddaa**(g)
tonight	i kväll	ee kvehl
tomorrow	i morgon	ee **morr**on
before Friday	före fredag	**fūr**rer **frāȳ**daa(g)
I want them as soon as possible.	Jag vill ha dem så snart som möjligt, tack.	yaa(g) vil haa dehm soa snaa^rt som **mury**lit tahk
Can you...this?	Skulle ni kunna... det här?	**skew**ler nee **kewn**ah... dāȳ(t) hær
mend/patch/stitch	laga/lappa/sy ihop	**laag**ah/**lahp**ah/**sēw** i**hōōp**
Can you sew on this button?	Skulle ni kunna sy i den här knappen?	**skew**ler nee **kewn**ah **sēw** ee dehn hær **knahp**ern
Can you get this stain out?	Kan ni få bort den här fläcken?	kahn nee foa bo^rt dehn hær **flehk**ern
Can this be invisibly mended?	Kan det här lagas utan att det syns?	kahn dāȳ(t) hær **laag**ahss **ēw**tahn aht dāȳ(t) sewnss
This isn't mine.	Det här är inte mitt.	dāȳ(t) hær ær **int**er mit
There's one piece missing.	Det fattas ett plagg.	dāȳ(t) **faht**ahss eht plahg
There's a hole in this.	Det är ett hål i det här.	dāȳ(t) ær eht hoal ee dāȳ(t) hær
Is my laundry ready?	Är min tvätt klar?	ær min tveht klaar

SHOPPING

Photography-Cameras

| I want an inexpensive camera. | **Jag skulle vilja ha en billig kamera.** | yaa(g) **skew**ler **vil**yah haa ehn **bil**li(g) **kaam**(er)rah |
| Show me the one in the window. | **Var snäll och visa mig den i fönstret.** | vaar snehl ok **vee**ssah may dehn ee **furn**strert |

Film

Basic still and home-movie exposure readings are given in English in the instructions with the roll.

Film sizes aren't always indicated the same way in Sweden as in the United States and Great Britain. The best thing to do when in difficulty is to show the shop assistant the kind of film you want, or to point to it in the box below. You'll also find the list of equivalents useful.

$110 = 13 \times 17$	$127 = 4 \times 4$
$120 = 6 \times 6$	$135 = 24 \times 36$
$126 = 26 \times 26$	$620 = 6 \times 6$

I'd like a...	**Jag skulle vilja ha...**	yaa(g) **skew**ler **vil**yah haa
film for this camera	**en film till den här kameran**	ehn film til dehn hæͬr **kaam**(er)rahn
colour film	**en färgfilm**	ehn **færy**film
black-and-white film	**en svart-vit film**	ehn svah^rt-veet film
Polaroid film	**en polaroid film**	ehn polahroo**eed** film
cartridge	**en filmpatron**	ehn **film**pahtrōͬon
20/36 exposures	**tjugo/trettiosex kort**	khēͬwgo/treht**issehks** koo^rt
this ASA/DIN number	**det här ASA/DIN numret**	dāͬy(t) hæͬr **aa**ssah/deen **newm**reht
fast film	**en grovkornig film**	ehn **grōͬov**kooͬr**nig film
fine grain	**en finkornig film**	ehn **feen**kooͬr**nig film
colour negatives	**färgnegativ**	**færy**nehgahteev
colour reversal	**en färgomvänd- ningsfilm**	ehn **færy**omvehnd- ningsfilm
colour slides	**färgdiapositiv**	**færy**diahpossitteev

FOR NUMBERS, see page 175.

artificial light-type	för inomhusljus	furr innomhewsyewss
daylight-type	för dagsljus	furr dahgssyewss
8-mm film	åtta millimeter film	ottah millimmayterr film
super 8	super åtta	sewperr ottah
16-mm film	sexton millimeter film	sehkston millimmayterr film

Processing

Does the price include processing?	Ingår framkall-ningen i priset?	ingoar frahmkahl-ningern ee preessert
Will you develop and print this?	Skulle ni kunna framkalla och göra kopior av den här?	skewler nee kewnah frahmkahlah ok yūrrah kopioor aav den hær
I want... prints of each negative.	Jag skall be att få... kopior av varje negativ.	yaa(g) skahl bay aht foa...kopioor aav vahryer nehgahteev
with a glossy finish	med glansig yta	mayd glahnsi(g) ewtah
with a matt finish	med matt yta	mayd maht ewtah
this size	den här storleken	dehn hær stoorlaykern
When will it be ready?	När blir det klart?	nær bleer day(t) klaart

Accessories

I want a/an/some...	Jag skall be att få...	yaa(g) skahl bay aht foa
cable release	en trådutlösare	ehn troadewtlurssahrer
camera case	ett kameraetui	eht kaam(er)rahehtewi
electronic flash	en elektronisk blixt	ehn ehlektroanisk blikst
exposure meter	en belysnings-mätare	ehn berlewssnings-maitahrer
filter	ett filter	eht filterr
polarizing	ett polaroid-filter	eht polahroeeed-filterr
red	rött	rurt
ultra-violet	ultra-violett	ewltrah-veeolleht
yellow	gult	gewlt
flash bulbs	blixtar	blikstahr
flash cubes	blixtkuber	blikstkewberr
lens	ett objektiv	eht obyehkteev
telephoto	ett teleobjektiv	eht taylerobyehkteev
wide-angle	ett vidvinkel-objektiv	eht veedvinkerl-obyehkteev

lens cap	ett linsskydd	eht linsshewd
lens cleaners	en linstorkare	ehn linsstorkahrer
tripod	ett stativ	eht stahteev

Broken

This camera doesn't work. Can you repair it?	Den här kameran fungerar inte. Kan ni laga den?	dehn hær kaam(er)rahn fewngayrahr inter. kahn nee laagah dehn
The film is jammed.	Filmen har hakat upp sig.	filmern haar haakaht ewp say
The knob won't turn.	Det går inte att vrida på knappen.	day(t) goar inter aht vreedah poa knahpern
There's something wrong with the...	Det är något fel på...	day(t) ær noagot fayl poa
automatic lens	den automatiska linsen	dehn ahtommaatiskah linssern
bellows	bälgen	behlyern
exposure counter	räkneverket	raiknerværkert
film feed	framdragningen	frahmdraagningern
flash contact	blixtkontakten	blikstkontahktern
lens	objektivet	obyehkteevert
lightmeter	ljusmätaren	yewsmaitahrern
rangefinder	belysningsmätaren	berlewsningsmaitahrern
shutter	slutaren	slewtahrern

Shooting

Do you mind if I take a few photographs?	Har ni något emot att jag tar ett par kort?	haar nee noagot ehmoot aht yaa(g) taar eht paar koo^rt
May I take a picture of you?	Kan jag få ta ett kort på er?	kahn yaa(g) foa taa eht koo^rt poa ayr
Please stand over there.	Var snäll och stå där borta.	vaar snehl ok stoa dær bo^rtah
I'll send you a print.	Jag skall sända er ett exemplar.	yaa(g) skahl sehndah ayr eht ehkssehmplaar

And, not forgetting yourself:

Would you mind taking my/our picture? Press this button.	Har ni något emot att ta ett kort på mig/oss? Tryck på den här knappen.	haar nee noagot ehmoot aht taa eht koo^rt poa may/oss? trewk poa dehn hær knahpern

Provisions

Here's a basic list of food and drink that you might
want on a picnic or for the occasional meal at home:

I'd like a/an/some...	Jag skall be att få...	yaa(g) skahl bāy aht foa
apples	några äpplen	noagrah ehplern
bananas	några bananer	noagrah bahnaanerr
biscuits (Br.)	några småkakor	noagrah smoakaakoor
bread	bröd	brūrd
butter	smör	smūrr
cakes	några kakor	noagrah kaakoor
candy	sötsaker	sūrtsaakerr
cheese	ost	oost
chocolate bar	en chokladkaka	ehn shoklaa(d)kaakah
coffee	kaffe	kahfer
cold cuts	kallskuret	kahlskēwrert
cookies	några småkakor	noagrah smoakaakoor
cooking-fat	stekfett	stāykfeht
crackers	ett paket kex	eht pahkāyt kehks
cream	grädde	grehder
crispbread	ett paket knäcke- bröd	eht pahkāyt knehker- brūrd
crisps	chips	khips
cucumbers	gurka	gewrkah
eggs	några ägg	noagrah ehg
fruit syrup (to be mixed with water)	en flaska saft	ehn flahskah sahft
ham	skinka	shinkah
hardtack	ett paket knäckebröd	eht pahkāyt knehkerbrūrd
ice-cream	glass	glahss
lemonade	sockerdricka	sokkerrdrikah
lemons	några citroner	noagrah sitrōōnerr
lettuce	grönsallad	grūrnsahlahd
liver paste	leverpastej	lāyverrpahstay
milk	mjölk	myurlk
mustard	senap	sāynahp
noodles	nudlar	newdlahr
oranges	några apelsiner	noagrah ahperlsseenerr
pepper	peppar	pehpahr
pickles	pickles	pikkerlss
potato chips	chips	khips
potatoes	potatisar	potaatissahr

salami	**salami**	sahlaami
salt	**salt**	sahlt
sandwiches	**smörgåsar**	smurrgoassahr
sausages	**korv**	korv
sugar	**socker**	sokkerr
sweets	**sötsaker**	sūrtsaakerr
tea	**te**	tay
tomatoes	**tomater**	tommaaterr

And don't forget...

aluminium foil	**foliepapper**	foolierpahperr
bottle opener	**en flasköppnare**	ehn flahskurpnahrer
corkscrew	**en korkskruv**	ehn korkskrewv
matches	**tändstickor**	tehnstikkor
paper napkins	**pappersservetter**	pahperr' særvehterr
paper towelling	**hushållspapper**	hewsholspahperr
plastic bags	**plastpåsar**	plahstpoassahr
tin (can) opener	**konservöppnare**	konsærvurpnahrer

Weights and measures

1 kilogram or kilo (kg.) = 1000 grams (g.)

| 100 g. = 3½ oz. | ½ kg. = 1 lb. 1½ oz. |
| 200 g. = 7 oz. | 1 kg. = 2 lb. 3 oz. |

1 oz. = 28.35 g.
1 lb. = 453.60 g.

1 litre (l.) = 0.88 imp. quarts = 1.06 U.S. quarts

| 1 imp. quart = 1.14 l. | 1 U.S. quart = 0.95 l. |
| 1 imp. gallon = 4.55 l. | 1 U.S. gallon = 3.8 l. |

---

box	**en ask**	ehn ask
can	**en burk**	ehn bewrk
carton	**en kartong**	ehn kah'tong
crate	**en spjällåda**	ehn spyailoadah
jar	**en kruka**	ehn krewkah
	(glasburk)	(glaasbewrk)
packet	**ett paket**	eht pahkayt
tin	**en burk**	ehn bewrk
tube	**en tub**	ehn tewb

Souvenirs

Among the souvenirs you may want to take home from Sweden, consider colourful textiles, woollen rugs, furniture, wood carvings and leather goods from Lappland.

The glassmaking industry, concentrated near the town of Växjö in southeastern Sweden, is a popular tourist attraction. It takes 15 years to become a skilled glassblower. You can see them at work.

Here are a few items for your shopping list:

ceramics	**keramik**	khehrah**meek**
coffee-set	**en kaffeservis**	ehn **kah**fers**ær**veess
Dala-horse	**en dalahäst**	ehn **daal**ahhehst
doll in national costume	**en docka i national- dräkt**	ehn **dokk**ah ee nahtsh**onn**aaldrehkt
glassware	**glas**	glaass
ashtray	**askkopp**	**ahs**kop
bowl	**skål**	skoal
glasses	**glas**	glaass
vase	**vas**	vaass
coloured	**färgat**	**fær**yaht
non-coloured	**ofärgat**	oofæryaht
crystal	**kristall**	kri**stahl**
engraved	**graverat**	grah**vay**raht
national costume for a boy/girl of 6	**en nationaldräkt för en 6-års pojke/flicka.**	ehn nahtsh**onn**aaldrehkt furr ehn 6-oa'ss **poyk**er/**flikk**ah
silver jewellery	**ett silversmycke**	eht **silv**err**smew**ker
textiles	**textilvaror**	tehks**teel**vaaroor
woollen rug	**en ryamatta**	ehn **rew**ahmahtah

Tobacconist's

Smoking is an expensive habit in Sweden, but virtually all international brands of cigarettes are available in tobacco shops and kiosks. Local cigarette brands are quite good, and Sweden is especially known for its quality pipe tobaccos.

I'd like a/an/some...	**Jag skall be att få...**	yaa(g) skahl bay aht foa
cigars	**några cigarrer**	noagrah siggahrerr
cigarette holder	**ett cigarrett-munstycke**	eht siggahrehtmewnstewker
cigarette lighter	**en cigarrettändare**	ehn siggahrehttehndahrer
flints	**stenar**	staynahr
lighter	**tändare**	tehndahrer
lighter fluid/ lighter gas	**bensin** **gas till en tändare**	behnsseen gaas til ehn tehndahrer
refill for a lighter	**refill till en tändare**	rerfeel til ehn tehndahrer
matches	**tändstickor**	tehnstikkoor
packet of...	**ett paket...**	eht pahkayt
packet of cigarettes	**ett paket cigarretter**	eht pahkayt siggahrehterr
pipe	**en pipa**	ehn peepah
pipe cleaners	**piprensare**	peeprehnsahrer
pipe tobacco	**piptobak**	peeptoobahk
pipe tool	**pipverktyg**	peepværktewg
tobacco pouch	**en tobakspung**	ehn toobahkspewng
wick	**en veke**	ehn vayker
Do you have any...	**Har ni några...?**	haar nee noagrah
American cigarettes	**amerikanska cigarretter**	ahm(er)rikaanskah siggahrehterr
English cigarettes	**engelska cigarretter**	ehngerlskah siggahrehterr
menthol cigarettes	**mentolcigarretter**	mehntolsiggahrehterr
I'll take two packets.	**Jag tar två paket, tack.**	yaa(g) taar tvoa pahkayt tahk
I'd like a carton.	**Jag skall be att få en limpa.**	yaa(g) skahl bay aht foa ehn limpah

| filter tipped | **med filter** | mayd filterr |
| without filter | **utan filter** | ewtahn filterr |

Your money: banks—currency

At larger banks there's sure to be someone who speaks English. In most tourist centres you'll find small currency-exchange offices (*växelkontor*—**veh**kserlkontoͪor) especially during the summer season. The exchange rate shouldn't vary much between them. Remember to take your passport along with you, as you may need it for identification.

Travellers' cheques and credit cards are widely accepted in tourist-orientated shops, hotels, restaurants etc. However, if you're exploring the countryside way off the beaten track you mustn't expect every little village store to be acquainted with them, or with foreign currency. The same goes for garages and service stations—only the main agency garages in the large cities will generally accept payment in travellers' cheques or by credit card.

Opening hours

Monday to Friday from 9.30 a.m. to 3.00 p.m. Some banks are also open two or three days a week between 4.30 and 6.00 p.m. They are closed all day Saturday, Sunday and on public holidays. In Stockholm, at the main railway station and Arlanda Airport, the exchange offices are open the whole day including weekends.

Monetary unit

The crown *(krona)* is the monetary unit of Sweden, Norway and Denmark, but its value differs in each country. The krona is divided into 100 *öre* (**ūr**rer). The abbreviation for crown is *kr*.

There are coins of 5 öre, 10 öre, 25 öre, 50 öre, 1 krona and 5 kronor, and notes of 5, 10, 50, 100, 1,000 and 10,000 kronor.

Before going

Where's the nearest bank/currency-exchange office?	**Var ligger närmaste bank/växelkontor?**	vaar **liggerr nærmahster** bahnk/**vehks**erlkont**ōōr**
Where can I cash a traveller's cheque?	**Var kan jag lösa in en resecheck?**	vaar kahn yaa(g) l**ū͞r**ssah in ehn r**ā͞y**sserkhek
Where's the Skandinaviska Enskilda Banken?	**Var ligger Skandinaviska Enskilda Banken?**	vaar **liggerr** skahndinn**aa**viskah **ā͞y**nshildah **bahn**kern

Inside

I want to change some dollars/pounds.	**Jag skulle vilja växla några dollar/pund.**	yaa(g) **skew**ler vilyah **vehks**lah n**oa**grah **doll**ahr/pewnd
What's the exchange rate?	**Vad är växelkursen?**	vaa(d) **ā͞r** **vehks**erlkew**ʳ**sern
Can you cash a personal cheque?	**Kan ni växla in en personlig check?**	kahn nee **vehks**lah in ehn pæ**ʳsō͞ō**nli(g) khehk
How long will it take to clear?	**Hur lång tid tar det?**	h**ē͞w**r long teed taar d**ā͞y**(t)
Can you wire my bank in...?	**Kan ni telegrafera till min bank...?**	kahn nee tehlergrah-f**ā͞y**rah til min bahnk ee
I have...	**Jag har...**	yaa(g) haar
a letter of credit	**ett kreditbrev**	eht kreh**deet**br**ā͞y**v
an introduction from...	**ett introduktionsbrev från...**	eht introddewk**shō͞ō**ns-br**ā͞y**v froan
a credit card	**ett kreditkort**	eht kreh**deet**koo**ʳ**t
I'm expecting some money from... Has it arrived yet?	**Jag väntar pengar från...Har de kommit?**	yaa(g) **vehn**tahr **peng**ahr froan... haar deh **komm**it
Please give me... notes (bills) and some small change.	**Ge mig...i sedlar och lite växel, tack.**	y**ā͞y** may...ee **sā͞y**dlahr ok **lee**ter **vehk**serl tahk
Give me...large notes and the rest in small notes.	**Ge mig...i stora sedlar och resten i små sedlar, tack.**	y**ā͞y** may...ee **stō͞ō**rah **sā͞y**dlahr ok **rehs**tern ee smoa **sā͞y**dlahr tahk
Could you please check that again?	**Var vänlig och kontrollera det där igen.**	vaar **vehn**li(g) ok kon-troll**ā͞y**rah day(t) d**ǣ**r iyehn

Depositing

I want to credit this to my account.	**Jag skulle vilja sätta in det här beloppet på mitt konto.**	yaa(g) **skew**ler vil**yah seh**tah in d$\overline{ay}$(t) hær berloppert poa mit konto
I want to credit this to Mr...'s account.	**Jag skulle vilja sätta in det här på Herr...s konto.**	yaa(g) **skew**ler vil**yah seh**tah in d$\overline{ay}$(t) hær poa hehr...ss konto
Where should I sign?	**Var skall jag skriva under?**	vaar skahl yaa(g) **skree**vah ewnderr

Currency converter

In a world of fluctuating exchange rates, we can offer no more than this do-it-yourself chart. You can get a card showing current èxchange rates from banks, travel agents and tourist offices. Why not fill in this chart, too, for handy reference?

Sweden	£	$
5 öre		
10 öre		
25 öre		
50 öre		
1 krona		
10 kronor		
50 kronor		
100 kronor		
500 kronor		
1000 kronor		
5000 kronor		

FOR NUMBERS, see page 175

At the post office

Post offices are indicated by the yellow letter P (Post). Mailboxes are painted yellow. Business hours are generally from 9 a.m. to 6 p.m., Monday to Friday, and from 9 a.m. to 1 p.m. on Saturdays. The main post office in Stockholm is open from 8 a.m. to 8 p.m. Monday to Friday, and 9 a.m. to 3 p.m. on Saturdays.

Where's the (nearest) post office?	**Var ligger (närmaste) post-kontor?**	vaar liggerr (nærmahster) postkontōōr
What window do I go to for stamps?	**I vilken lucka kan jag köpa frimärken?**	ee vilkern lewkah kahn yaa(g) khūrpah freemærkern
At which counter can I cash an international money order?	**I vilken lucka kan jag kvittera ut en internationell postanvisning?**	ee vilkern lewkah kahn yaa(g) kvittāyrah ēwt ehn interrnahtshonnehl postahnveesning
I want some stamps, please.	**Jag skulle vilja ha några frimärken.**	yaa(g) skewler vilyah haa noagrah freemærkern
I want...90-öre stamps and... 1-crown stamps.	**Jag skall be att få ...90-öres-fri-märken och... 1-kronas.**	yaa(g) skahl bāy aht foa ...90-ūrrerss freemærkern ok...1-krōōnahs
What's the postage for a letter to England?	**Vad är portot för ett brev till England?**	vaa(d) ær po^rtot fūrr eht brāyv til ehnglahnd
What's the postage for a postcard to the USA?	**Vad är portot för ett vykort till USA?**	vaa(d) ær po^rtot fūrr eht vēwkoo^rt til ēwehssaa
I want to send this parcel.	**Jag skulle vilja skicka det här paketet.**	yaa(g) skewler vilyah shikkah dāy(t) hær pahkāytert
Do I need to fill in a customs declaration?	**Behöver jag fylla i en tulldeklara-tionsblankett?**	berhūrverr yaa(g) fewlah ee ehn tewldeh-klahrahshōōnsblahnkeht

Where's the mail-box?	**Var är brevlådan?**	vaar ær **brayv**loadahn
I want to send this by...	**Jag vill sända det här...**	yaa(g) vil **sehn**dah day(t) hær
airmail	**med flyg**	mayd flewg
express (special delivery)	**express**	ehk**sprehss**
registered mail	**rekommenderat**	rehkommern**day**raht
surface mail	**med vanlig post**	mayd **vaan**li(g) post
small parcel	**som brevpaket**	som **brayv**pahkayt
Where's the poste restante (general delivery)?	**Var är poste restanteluckan?**	vaar ær post reh**stahn**ter-lewkahn
Is there any mail for me? My name is...	**Finns det någon post till mig? Mitt namn är...**	finss day(t) **noa**gon post til may? mit nahmn ær
Here's my passport.	**Här är mitt pass.**	hær ær mit pahss

FRIMÄRKEN	STAMPS
PAKET	PARCELS
UTBETALNINGAR	MONEY ORDERS

Telegrams

Where's the (nearest) telegraph office?	**Var ligger (närmaste) telegrafstation?**	vaar **ligg**err (**nær**mahster) tehler**graaf**stahshoon
I want to send a telegram. May I please have a form?	**Jag skulle vilja sända ett telegram. Kan jag få en blankett, tack?**	yaa(g) **skew**ler **vil**yah **sehn**dah eht tehler**grahm**. kahn yaa(g) foa ehn blahn**keht** tahk
How much is it per word?	**Vad kostar det per ord?**	vaa(d) **kos**tahr day(t) pær oo'rd
I'd like to reverse the charges.	**Mottagaren betalar.**	**moo**taagahrern ber**taa**lahr
I'd like to send a night-rate telegram.	**Jag skulle vilja sända ett brevtelegram.**	yaa(g) **skew**ler **vil**yah **sehn**dah eht **brayv**tehlergram

Telephoning

Sweden's advanced telephone system permits you to dial directly to all places within the country as well as to a large number of other countries.

Note: Stockholm has both 6- and 7-digit numbers.

General

Where's there a public telephone?	**Var finns det en telefonkiosk?**	vaar finss day(t) ehn tehlerfoankhiosk
May I use your phone?	**Kan jag få låna er telefon?**	kahn yaa(g) foa loanah ayr tehlerfoan
Do you have a telephone directory for Helsingborg?	**Har ni en katalog över Helsingborg?**	haar nee ehn kahtahloag ūrverr hehlsingbory
Can you help me get this number?	**Kan ni hjälpa mig att komma till det här numret?**	kahn nee yehlpah may aht kommah til day(t) hær newmrert

Operator

Do you speak English?	**Talar ni engelska?**	taalahr nee ehngerlskah
Good morning, I want...	**Goddag. Jag skulle vilja komma till...**	goddaag. yaa(g) skewler vilyah kommah til
Can I dial direct?	**Kan jag slå direkt?**	kahn yaa(g) sloa dirrehkt
I want to place a personal (person-to-person) call.	**Jag skulle vilja beställa ett personligt samtal.**	yaa(g) skewler vilyah berstehlah eht pærsoonlit sahmtaal
I want to reverse the charges.	**Samtalet skall betalas av mottagaren.**	sahmtaalert skahl bertaalahss aav mootaagahrern
Will you tell me the cost of the call afterwards?	**Kan ni meddela mig efteråt vad samtalet kostade?**	kahn nee mayderlah may ehfterroat vaa(d) sahmtaalert kostahder

FOR NUMBERS, see page 175.

Speaking

Hello. This is... speaking.	**Hallå. Det här är...**	hahloa. dāy(t) hǟr ǟr
I want to speak to...	**Jag skall be att få tala med...**	yaa(g) skahl bay aht foa taalah māyd
Would you put me through to...?	**Kan ni koppla mig till...?**	kahn nee koplah may til
I want extension...	**Jag skall be att få anknytning...**	yaa(g) skahl bay aht foa ahnknēwtning

Bad luck

Would you please try again later?	**Kan ni försöka lite senare, tack?**	kahn nee furˡsūrkah leeter saynahrer tahk
Operator, you gave me the wrong number.	**Jag tror ni gav mig fel nummer.**	yaa(g) trōor nee gaav may fāyl newmerr
Operator, we were cut off.	**Samtalet blev brutet.**	sahmtaalert blāyv brēwtert
The connection was bad.	**Linjen var dålig.**	linyern vaar doali(g)
Would you please try the number again?	**Skulle ni kunna försöka det här numret igen?**	skewler nee kewnah furˡssūrkah dāy(t) hǟr newmrert iyehn

---

Telephone alphabet

A	**Adam**	aadahm	P	**Peter**	pāyterr
B	**Bertil**	bǣˡtil	Q	**Quintus**	kvintewss
C	**Cesar**	sāyssahr	R	**Rudolf**	rēwdolf
D	**David**	daavid	S	**Sigurd**	seegewˡd
E	**Erik**	āyrik	T	**Tore**	tōorer
F	**Filip**	feelip	U	**Urban**	ewrbahn
G	**Gustav**	gewstahv	V	**Viktor**	viktor
H	**Helge**	hehlger	W	**Wilhelm**	vilhehlm
I	**Ivar**	eevahr	X	**Xerxes**	ksehrksehs
J	**Johan**	yōohahn	Y	**Yngve**	ewngver
K	**Kalle**	kahler	Z	**Zeta**	sāytah
L	**Ludwig**	lewdvig	Å	**Åke**	oaker
M	**Martin**	mahˡtin	Ä	**Ärlig**	ǣrlig
N	**Niklas**	niklahss	Ö	**Östen**	urstern
O	**Olof**	ōolov			

Not there

When will he/she be back?	**När kommer han/ hon tillbaka?**	nær kommerr hahn/hon tilbaakah
Will you tell him/her I called? My name's...	**Skulle ni kunna meddela honom/ henne att jag ringt? Mitt namn är...**	skewler nee kewnah mayderlah honnom/ hehner aht yaa(g) ringt. mit nahmn ær
Would you ask him/ her to call me?	**Skulle ni kunna be honom/henne ringa mig?**	skewler nee kewnah bay honnom/hehner ringah may
Would you please take a message?	**Skulle ni kunna ta ett meddelande?**	skewler nee kewnah taa eht mayderlahnder

Charges

What was the cost of that call?	**Vad kostar samtalet?**	vaa(d) kostahr sahmtaalert
I want to pay for the call.	**Jag skulle vilja betala samtalet.**	yaa(g) skewler vilyah bertaalah sahmtaalert

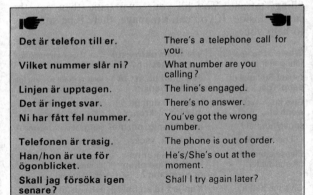

Det är telefon till er.	There's a telephone call for you.
Vilket nummer slår ni?	What number are you calling?
Linjen är upptagen.	The line's engaged.
Det är inget svar.	There's no answer.
Ni har fått fel nummer.	You've got the wrong number.
Telefonen är trasig.	The phone is out of order.
Han/hon är ute för ögonblicket.	He's/She's out at the moment.
Skall jag försöka igen senare?	Shall I try again later?

The car

This section is entirely devoted to motoring. It's been divided into three parts:

Part A (pages 142-145) contains the phrases you'll need at the filling station and when asking the way.

Part B (pages 146-149) contains general advice on motoring in Sweden, hints and regulations.

Part C (pages 150-159) is concerned with the practical details of breakdown and accidents. It includes a list of car parts and of the things that may go wrong with them. All you have to do is to show the list to the mechanic and get him to point to the repairs and items required.

Part A—Filling station

Self-service has become almost universal at Swedish filling stations. You fill your own tank, then pay the cashier inside. If you can't manage, there'll be someone to help you.

Where's the nearest filling station?	**Var finns närmaste bensinstation?**	vaar finss **nær**mahster behn**sseen**stahshoon
I want 30 litres of petrol (gas), please.	**Jag skall be att få 30 liter bensin.**	yaa(g) skahl bay aht foa 30 **lee**terr behn**sseen**
Give me ... crowns' worth of...	**Var snäll och ge mig för ... kronor...**	vaar snehl ok yay may furr ... **kroo**noor
super/normal	**högoktanig/normal**	**hur**goktaanig/**nor**maal
Fill her up, please.	**Full tank, tack.**	fewl tahnk tahk
Please check the oil and water.	**Skulle ni kunna kontrollera oljan och vattnet?**	**skew**ler nee **kew**nah kontrol**lay**rah **ol**yahn ok **vaht**nert
Give me half a litre of oil.	**Kan jag få en halv liter olja, tack?**	kahn yaa(g) foa ehn hahlv **lee**terr **ol**yah tahk

FOR NUMBERS, see page 175

Fill up the battery with distilled water.	**Fyll på vatten i batteriet, tack.**	fewl poa **vahtern** ee bahterriert tahk
Check the brake fluid.	**Kan ni kolla broms-vätskan, tack?**	kahn nee kollah **broms-**vehtskahn tahk
Put in some anti-freeze, please.	**Var snäll och häll i lite glykol.**	vaar snehl ok hehl ee leeter glewkoal

Fluid measures					
litres	imp. gal.	U.S. gal.	litres	imp. gal.	U.S. gal.
5	1.1	1.3	30	6.6	7.8
10	2.2	2.6	35	7.7	9.1
15	3.3	3.9	40	8.8	10.4
20	4.4	5.2	45	9.9	11.7
25	5.5	6.5	50	11.0	13.0

Would you check the tires?	**Skulle ni kunna kontrollera däcken?**	skewler nee kewnah kontrollāyrah dehkern
Please check the spare tire, too.	**Var snäll och kontrollera reserv-däcket också.**	vaar snehl ok kontro-llāyrah rehssærv-dehkert oksoa
1.6 front, 1.8 rear	**1 komma 6 fram, 1 komma 8 bak.**	1 kommah 6 frahm 1 kommah 8 baak

Tire pressure is measured in Sweden in kilograms per square centimetre. The following conversion chart will make sure your tires get the treatment they deserve. Just point to the pressures required.

Tire pressure			
lb./sq. in.	kg./cm^2	lb./sq. in.	kg./cm^2
10	0.7	26	1.8
12	0.8	27	1.9
15	1.1	28	2.0
18	1.3	30	2.1
20	1.4	33	2.3
21	1.5	36	2.5
23	1.6	38	2.7
24	1.7	40	2.8

Can you mend this puncture (fix this flat)?	**Skulle ni kunna laga den här punkteringen?**	skewler nee kewnah laagah dehn hær pewnktäyringern
Would you please change this tire?	**Skulle ni kunna byta det här däcket?**	skewler nee kewnah bewtah dāy(t) hær dehkert
Would you clean the windscreen (windshield)?	**Skulle ni kunna torka av vindrutan?**	skewler nee kewnah torkah aav vin(d)-rewtahn
I want maintenance and lubrication service.	**Kan ni rundsmörja bilen, tack?**	kahn nee rewn(d)-smurryah beelern tahk
Have you a road map of this district?	**Har ni någon vägkarta?**	haar nee noagon vaigkaartah
I've run out of petrol (gas) at... Could you please help me?	**Jag har fått bensinstopp vid... Skulle ni kunna hjälpa mig?**	yaa(g) haar fot behn-sseenstop veed... skewler nee kewnah yehlpah may

Asking the way—Street directions

Excuse me. Do you speak English?	**Förlåt mig, talar ni engelska?**	fur'loat may taalahr nee ehngerlskah
Can you tell me the way to...?	**Kan ni säga mig hur man kommer till...?**	kahn nee sehyah may hewr mahn kommerr til

Miles into kilometres									
1 mile = 1.609 kilometres (km.)									
miles	10	20	30	40	50	60	70	80	90	100
km.	16	32	48	64	80	97	113	129	145	161

Kilometres into miles												
1 kilometre (km. = 0.62 miles)												
km.	10	20	30	40	50	60	70	80	90	100	110	120	130
miles	6	12	19	25	31	37	44	50	56	62	68	75	81

Where does this road lead to?	**Vart går den här vägen?**	vah[r]t goar dehn hǣr **vai**gern
Are we on the right road for...?	**Är det här vägen till...?**	ǣr dāy(t) hǣr **vai**gern til
How far is the next village?	**Hur långt är det till nästa samhälle?**	hēwr longt ǣr dāy(t) til **neh**stah **sahm**hehler
How far is it to... from here?	**Hur långt är det till ...härifrån?**	hēwr longt ǣr dāy(t) til...hǣrifroan
Where can I find this address?	**Hur kommer jag till den här adressen?**	hēwr **kom**merr yaa(g) til dehn hǣr ah**dreh**ssern
Can you show me on the map where I am?	**Kan ni visa mig på kartan var jag befinner mig, tack?**	kahn nee **vee**ssah may poa **kaa**[r]tahn vaar yaa(g) ber**fin**nerr may tahk
Can you show me on the map where...is?	**Kan ni visa mig på kartan, var... ligger, tack?**	kahn nee **vee**ssah may poa **kaa**[r]tahn vaar... **lig**gerr tahk
Can I park there?	**Kan jag parkera där?**	kahn yaa(g) pahr**kāy**rah dǣr
Is that a one-way street?	**Är det en enkel- riktad gata?**	ǣr dāy(t) ehn **ehn**kerl- riktahd **gaa**tah

---

☞   ☜

Ni har kört fel.	You're on the wrong road.
Kör rakt fram.	Go straight ahead.
Det är därnere till...	It's down there on the...
vänster/höger	left/right
Det är för långt att gå dit.	It's too far to walk.
Ta buss nummer...	Catch bus number...
Kör till första/andra korsningen.	Go to the first/second crossroads.
Ta av till vänster vid trafikljusen.	Turn left at the traffic lights.
Ta av till höger vid gathörnet.	Turn right at the corner.

Part B—Customs—Documentation

You'll require the following documents to enter Sweden with your car:

    passport
    national or international driving licence
    car registration papers
    national identity sticker
    green card or other internationally valid third party insurance

Traffic drives on the right in Sweden. All vehicles (including motorcycles) must have dipped headlights switched on at all times, even in broad daylight. Crash helmets are compulsory for drivers and passengers on motorcycles and scooters.

Safety-belts are compulsory for driver and front-seat passenger, and you must have a red warning triangle with you. Recommended: parking lamp.

Warning: Swedish law does not tolerate inebriated drivers. One strong beer is enough to land you in serious trouble.

Here's my...	Här är mitt...	hær ær mit
(international) driving licence	(internationella) körkort	(interrnahtshonnehlah) khurᵇkooᵇt
green card	gröna kort	grürnah kooᵇt
log book (registration card)	besiktningsinstrument	bersiktningsinstrewmehnt
passport	pass	pahss
I've nothing to declare.	Jag har ingenting att deklarera.	yaa(g) haar ingernting aht dehklahrāyrah
I've...	Jag har...	yaa(g) haar
a carton of cigarettes	en limpa cigarretter	ehn limpah siggahrehterr
a bottle of whisky	en flaska whisky	ehn flahskah wiski
a bottle of wine	en flaska vin	ehn flahskah veen
We're staying for...	Vi skall stanna...	vee skahl stahnah
a week	en vecka	ehn vehkah
two weeks	två veckor	tvoa vehkoor
a month	en månad	ehn moanahd

Roads

Most Swedish roads are very good, though only a small proportion are motorways (expressways). Parking is forbidden at the side of main roads, but many off-the-road parking spots are provided. Speed limits are marked on all roads.

Motorways, numbered with the prefix "E", are called *Europavägar,* or European Highways. Two-digit numbers mark main national roads (*Riksvägar*—**riks**vaigahr). Three-digit numbers identify second and third-class roads.

In winter you'll need good snow tires. In the northern part of Sweden you'll drive on hard-packed snow. These winter roads *(vintervägar)* are not at all slippery—they are, in fact, excellent highways.

In Sweden's major cities a special service helps arriving tourists to find their way. "Tourist pilots" on motor scooters, armed with maps and brochures and speaking several languages, can help you through the urban traffic. The service is free.

Speed limits

Maximum speed limits are indicated by signs on all roads.

110 km/hour	motorways and main national roads
90 km/hour	main roads
70 km/hour	minor roads
50 km/hour	built-up areas

Note that caravans equipped with brakes are limited to 70 km/hour, and those without brakes to 40 km/hour.

CAR—INFORMATION

I didn't see the sign/light.	Jag såg inte skylten/ljuset.	yaa(g) soag inter shewltern/yēwssert
The light was green.	Ljuset var grönt.	yēwssert vaar grūrnt
I'm sorry. I don't speak much Swedish.	Tyvärr talar jag inte mycket svenska.	tewvær taalahr yaa(g) inter mewker(t) svehnskah
I don't understand.	Jag förstår inte.	yaa(g) furrstoar inter
How much is the fine?	Hur höga är böterna?	hēwr hūrgah ær būrterrnah

Parking

The police are normally lenient with tourists, but don't push your luck. Parking fines are high in Sweden.

Once you've parked your car and become a pedestrian, be sure to use the marked crossings and follow the signal lights. Jay-walkers are fined, too.

Excuse me. May I park here?	Förlåt mig. Får man parkera här?	furrloat may. foar mahn pahrkāyrah hær
How long may I park here?	Hur länge får man stå här?	hēwr lehnger foar mahn stoa hær
What's the charge for parking here?	Vad kostar det att parkera här?	vaa(d) kostahr dāy(t) aht pahrkāyrah hær
Do I have to leave my lights on?	Bör jag låta ljusen stå på?	būrr yaa(g) loatah yēwssern stoa poa
Excuse me. Do you have some change for the parking meter?	Förlåt mig. Ni har inte lite växel till parkerings-automaten?	furrloat may nee haar inter leeter vehkserl til pahrkāyringsahtommaatern

Swedish road signs

In addition to the internationally standardized road signs
(see pages 160-161), Sweden uses some written signs and
notices of its own, sometimes in conjunction with picto-
graphs, sometimes alone. Study this page beforehand so
you're prepared for them.

BADPLATS	Swimming pool, beach
CYKELVÄG	Cycle path
EJ MOTORFORDON	No motor vehicles
FARLIG KURVA	Dangerous bend
HUVUDLED	Main road
HÅLL TILL HÖGER (or HÅLL TILL H)	Keep to the right
HÖGSTA TILLÅTNA HASTIGHET...KM	Speed limit...km
KORSANDE SKIDSPÅR	Ski-track merging
KORSANDE TIMMERVÄG	Lumber-track merging
KÖR SAKTA	Drive slowly
MOTORVÄG	Motorway (expressway)
MÖTESPLATS	Passing place
NEDSATT HÖRSEL	Caution: deaf people
NEDSATT SYN	Caution: blind people
OMVÄG	Detour
PARKERING	Parking
PRIVAT VÄG	Private road
RASTPLATS	Roadside picnic site
RIDVÄG	Horse-riding path
RÖDA KORSETS HJÄLP-STATION	Red-Cross first-aid post
SKOLA	School
SLIRIG KÖRBANA	Slippery road
STOPP	Stop
STOPP FÖR TULL	Customs: Stop
TJÄLSKOTT	Potholes due to frost
VANDRARHEM	Hikers' hostel
VÄGARBETE	Roadworks ahead
ÅTERVÄNDSVÄG/GATA	No through road

CAR—INFORMATION

Part C—Accidents

This section is confined to immediate aid. The legal problems of responsibility and settlement can be taken care of at a later stage.

Your first concern will be for the injured.

Is anyone hurt?	**Är någon skadad?**	ǣr **noa**gon **skaa**dahd
Don't move.	**Rör er inte.**	rurr **āȳr** inter
It's all right, don't worry.	**Oroa er inte. Det kommer att gå bra.**	**ōō**rooah **āȳr** inter. dāȳ(t) kommerr aht goa braa
Where's the nearest telephone?	**Var finns närmaste telefon?**	vaar finss **nærr**mahster tehler**foan**
Can I use your phone? There's been an accident.	**Kan jag få låna er telefon? Det har hänt en olycka.**	kahn yaa(g) foa **loa**nah **āȳr** tehler**foan**? dāȳ(t) haar hehnt ehn **ōō**lewkah
Call a doctor/an ambulance quickly.	**Ring genast efter en läkare/ambulans.**	ring **yāȳ**nahst **ehf**terr ehn ehn **lai**kahrer/ahm-bew**lahnss**
There are people injured.	**Några är skadade.**	**noa**grah ǣr **skaa**dahder
Help me get them out of the car.	**Hjälp mig att få dem ur bilen.**	yehlp may aht foa dehm **ēwr bee**lern

Police—Exchange of information

Please call the police.	**Var snäll och ring efter polisen.**	vaar snehl ok ring **ehf**terr poleessern
There's been an accident.	**Det har hänt en olycka.**	dāȳ(t) haar hehnt ehn **ōō**lewkah
It's about 2 kilometres from...	**Det är ca. 2 kilometer från...**	dāȳ(t) ǣr cirkah 2 khillom**māȳ**terr froan
I'm on the Malmö-Stockholm road, 25 km from Gränna.	**Jag är på vägen mellan Malmö och Stockholm, 25 km från Gränna.**	yaa(g) ǣr poa **vai**gern **meh**lan **mahl**mur ok **stokk**holm 25 khillo-**māȳ**terr.froan **greh**nah
Here's my name and address.	**Här är mitt namn och min adress.**	hǣr ǣr mit nahmn ok min ah**drehss**

| Would you mind acting as a witness? | **Har ni något emot att vara mitt vittne?** | haar nee noagot ehmoot aht vaarah mit vitner |
| I'd like an interpreter. | **Jag skulle vilja ha en tolk.** | yaa(g) skewler vilyah haa ehn tolk |

Remember to put out a red warning triangle if your car is out of action or impeding traffic.

Breakdown

...and that's what we'll do with this section: break it down into four phases.

1. *On the road*
   You ask where the nearest garage is.

2. *At the garage*
   You tell the mechanic what's wrong.

3. *Finding the trouble*
   He tells you what he thinks needs doing.

4. *Getting it repaired*
   You tell him to repair it and, once that's over, settle the account (or argue about it).

Phase 1—On the road

Where's the nearest garage?	**Var ligger närmaste verkstad?**	vaar liggerr nærmahster værkstaa(d)
Excuse me, my car has broken down. May I use your phone?	**Förlåt mig, jag har fått motorstopp. Kan jag få låna telefonen?**	fur(r)loat may yaa(g) haar fot mootorstop. kahn yaa(g) foa loanah tehlerfoanern
What's the telephone number of the nearest garage?	**Vad är det för nummer till närmaste verkstad?**	vaa(d) ær day(t) fürr newmerr til nærmahster værkstaa(d)
I've had a breakdown at...	**Jag fick motorstopp på...**	yaa(g) fik mootorstop poa

Can you send a mechanic?	**Kan ni sända en mekaniker?**	kahn nee **sehn**dah ehn meh**kaa**nikkerr
Can you send a truck to tow my car?	**Kan ni sända en bärgningsbil?**	kahn nee **sehn**dah ehn b**ǣry**ningsbeel
How long will you be?	**Hur lång tid kommer det att ta?**	hēwr long teed **kom**merr dāȳ(t) aht taa

Phase 2—At the garage

Can you help me?	**Kan ni hjälpa mig?**	kahn nee **yehl**pah may
I don't know what's wrong with it.	**Jag vet inte var felet ligger.**	yaa(g) vāȳt inter vaar **fāȳ**lert liggerr
I think there's something wrong with the...	**Jag tror det är något fel på...**	yaa(g) trōōr dāȳ(t) ǣr **noa**got fāȳl poa
acceleration	**accelerations-förmågan**	ahkserlehrah**shōōns**-furrmoagahn
air conditioning	**ventilationen**	vehntillah**shōō**nern
axle	**hjulaxeln**	**yēw**lahkserln
battery	**batteriet**	bahter**ri**ert
brakes	**bromsarna**	**broms**ah^rnah
choke	**choken**	**khoa**kern
clutch	**kopplingen**	**kop**lingern
cooling system	**kylsystemet**	**khēwl**sewstāȳmert
dip (dimmer) switch	**avbländningen**	**aav**blehndningern
direction indicator	**körriktningsvisaren**	kh**ūr**riktningsveessahrern
distributor	**fördelardosan**	fur^r**dāȳ**lahrdoossahn
door	**dörren**	**durr**ern
dynamo	**generatorn**	yehnerr**raa**to^rn
electrical system	**det elektriska systemet**	dāȳ(t) eh**lehk**triskah sewstāȳmert
engine	**motorn**	**mōō**to^rn
fan	**fläkten**	**flehk**tern
fan belt	**fläktremmen**	**flehk**trehmern
fuel feed	**oljetillförseln**	**ol**yertilfur^rserln
gears	**växlarna**	**vehks**lah^rnah
generator	**generatorn**	yehnerr**raa**to^rn
heating	**värmesystemet**	**vǣr**mersewstāȳmert
horn	**signalhornet**	singn**aal**hōō^rnert
ignition system	**tändningen**	**tehnd**ningern
injection system	**injektions-systemet**	inyehk**shōōns**sewstāȳmert
lights	**ljusen**	**yēw**ssern
brake lights	**bromsljusen**	broms**yēw**ssern
headlights	**strålkastarna**	**stroal**kahstah^rnah

English	Swedish	Pronunciation
rear (tail) lights	**baklyktorna**	baaklewktoo'nah
reversing (backup) lights	**backljusen**	bahkyewssern
oil system	**oljesystemet**	olyersewstaymert
overdrive	**överväxeln**	ūrverrvehkserln
radiator	**kylaren**	khewlahrern
seat	**sätet**	saitert
seat belt	**säkerhetsbältet**	saikerrhaytsbehltert
silencer (muffler)	**ljuddämparen**	yewdehmpahrern
speedometer	**hastighets-mätaren**	hahstighaytsmai-tahrern
starter motor	**startmotorn**	stah'tmooto'n
steering	**styrinrättningen**	stewrinrehtningern
suspension	**fjädringen**	fyaidringern
transmission	**kraftöverföringen**	krahftūrverfurringern
turn signal	**körriktnings-visaren**	kūrriktnings-veessahrern
wheels	**hjulen**	yewlern
wipers	**vindrutetorkarna**	vindrewtertorkah'nah

LEFT	RIGHT	FRONT	BACK
VÄNSTER	**HÖGER**	**FRAM**	**BAK**
(vehnsterr)	(hūrgerr)	(frahm)	(baak)

It's...

English	Swedish	Pronunciation
backfiring	**eftertänder**	ehfterrtehnderr
bad	**dåligt**	doali(g)t
blowing	**förbränt**	furrbrehnt
blown	**sprängt**	sprehngt
broken	**avbrutet**	aavbrewtert
burnt	**bränt**	brehnt
chafing	**sliter/skaver**	sleeterr/skaaverr
cracked	**sprucket**	sprewkert
defective	**trasigt**	traasist
disconnected	**har lossat**	haar lossaht
dry	**torrt**	to't
frozen	**fruset**	frewssert
jammed	**har hakat upp sig**	haar haakaht ewp say
jerking	**går ojämt**	goar ooyehmt
knocking	**knackar**	knahkahr
leaking	**läcker**	lehkerr
loose	**är löst**	ær lūrsst
noisy	**bullrigt**	bewlrit
overheating	**överhettat**	ūrverrhehtaht
slack	**slakt**	slaakt

slipping	**slirar**	**slee**rahr
split	**sprucket**	**sprew**kert
stuck	**fast**	fahst
vibrating	**vibrerar**	vibrayrahr
weak	**svagt**	svaagt
The car won't start.	**Bilen startar inte.**	beelern stah^rtahr inter
The car won't pull.	**Bilen accelererar inte.**	beelern ahkserlehrayrahr inter
The car is making a funny noise.	**Det är något konstigt ljud.**	day(t) är noagot konstit yewd
It's locked and the keys are inside.	**Bilen är låst och nycklarna ligger inuti.**	beelern är loast ok newklah^rnah liggerr innewti
The radiator is leaking.	**Kylaren läcker.**	khewlahrern lehkerr
The clutch engages too quickly.	**Kopplingen tar för snabbt.**	koplingern taar furr snahbt
I can't engage first/reverse gear.	**Jag får inte in ettan/backen.**	yaa(g) foar inter in ehtahn/bahkern
The steering wheel's vibrating.	**Ratten vibrerar.**	rahtern vibrayrahr
The...needs adjusting.	**...behöver justeras.**	...berhurver shewstayrahss
brake	**kopplingen**	koplingern
clutch	**bromsarna**	bromsah^rnah
idling	**tomgången**	tomgongern

Now that you've explained what's wrong, you'll want to know how long it'll take to repair it and make your arrangements accordingly.

How long will it take to find out what's wrong?	**Hur lång tid kommer det att ta att hitta felet?**	hewr long teed kommerr day(t) aht taa aht hittah faylert
How long will it take to repair?	**Hur lång tid kommer det att ta att laga felet?**	hewr long teed kommerr day(t) aht taa aht laagah faylert
Suppose I come back in half an hour?	**Kan jag komma tillbaka om en halvtimme?**	kahn yaa(g) kommah tilbaakah om ehn hahlvtimmer

Can you give me a lift into town?	**Skulle ni kunna ge mig skjuts till stan?**	skewler nee kewnah yay may shew(t)ss til staan
Is there a place to stay nearby?	**Kan jag bo någon-stans i närheten?**	kahn yaa(g) bōō noagonstahnss ee nærhaytern
May I use your phone?	**Skulle jag kunna få låna er telefon?**	skewler yaa(g) kewnah foa loanah āyr tehlerfoan

Phase 3—Finding the trouble

Now it's up to the mechanic to pinpoint the trouble and repair it. Just hand him the book and point to the text in Swedish below.

Var vänlig och se på följande alfabetiska lista och peka på den trasiga delen. Om er kund vill veta var felet ligger, visa honom den engelska termen (bruten, kort-slutning, etc.)*.

avbländningen	dip (dimmer) switch
avgasröret	exhaust pipe
axeln	shaft
batteriet	battery
batterivätskan	battery fluid
bensinmätaren	fuel gauge
bensinpumpen	pump
bensintanken	tank
bensintillförseln	feed
blandningen	mixture
bromsbelägget	brake lining
bromsen	brake
bromstrumman	brake drum
brytarspetsarna	points
bult	bolt
chassit	chassis
choken	choke
cylinderlocket	cylinder head
cylinderlockpackningen	cylinder head gasket

* Please look at the following alphabetical list and point to the defective item. If your customer wants to know what's wrong with it, pick out the applicable term (broken, short-circuited etc.).

elektriska systemet	electrical system
filtret	filter
fjädern	spring
fjädringen	suspension
flottören (på förgasaren)	float
fläkten	fan
fläktremmen	fan belt
fördelardosan	distributor
fördelarledningarna	distributor leads
förgasaren	carburettor
generatorn	dynamo (generator)
hjulen	wheels
hydraliska bromssystemet	hydraulic brake system
injektionspumpen	injection pump
kabeln	cable
kablarna	wiring
kamaxeln	camshaft
kardanaxeln	propeller shaft
kardanknuten	universal joint
kolven	piston
kondensatorn	condenser
kontakten	contact
kopplingen	clutch
kopplingspedalen	clutch pedal
kopplingsskivan	clutch plate
kuggarna	teeth
kuggstångsstyrdriften	rack and pinion
kullagren	main bearing
kraftöverföringen	transmission
kylaren	radiator
kylsystemet	cooling system
lagerhuset	casing
lagren	bearing
ledningen	connection
ljuddämparen	silencer (muffler)
luftfiltret	air filter
membranet	diaphragm
motorblocket	block
motorn	engine
mätaren	gauge
oljefiltret	oil filter
oljekylaren	cooler
oljepumpen	pump
oljesumpen	sump (oil pan)
packningen	joint (packing)
pumpen	pump

rattrören	steering column (post)
reflexanordningen	reflector
relät	relay
ringarna	rings
sladdarna	leads
spolen	coil
stabilisatorn	stabilizer
startarmaturet	starter armature
startmotorn	starter motor
styrningen	steering
styrsnäckan	steering-box
stötdämparen	shock-absorber
stötstängerna	tappet
svänghjulet	flywheel
termostaten	thermostat
tändspolen	ignition coil
tändstiften	sparking plugs
varningslampan	warning lamp
vattenpumpen	water pump
ventilationen	air-conditioning
ventilen	valve
vevaxeln	crankshaft
vevhuset	crankcase
vevstaken	connecting (piston) rod
växellådan	gear box
växelspaken	gear lever

Följande lista innehåller ord som inte bara beskriver var felet ligger utan också vad som behöver göras*.

att balansera	to balance
att belägga	to reline
bruten	broken
bränd	burnt
att byta	to change
att byta ut	to replace
fet blandning	rich
frusen	frozen
att fästa	to tighten
för varm	overheating
förbränd	blowing
glapp	play
har hakat upp sig	jammed
har lossnat	disconnected

* The following list contains words which describe what's wrong as well as what may need to be done.

hög	high
att justera	to adjust
kortslutning	short-circuited
att köra in	to grind in
att ladda	to charge
laddar inte	not charging
att lossa	to loosen
låg	low
läcker	leaking
lös	loose
att rengöra	to clean
slak	slack
slirar	slipping
sliten	worn
smutsig	dirty
snabb	quick
sprucken	cracked
sprängd	blown
svag	weak
sönderrostad	corroded
att ta isär	to strip down
torr	dry
trasig	defective
tänder inte	misfiring
att tömma	to bleed
urgröpt	pitted

Phase 4—Getting it repaired

Have you found the trouble?	**Har ni hittat felet?**	haar nee hittaht **fay**lert
Is that serious?	**Är det allvarligt?**	ær d$\overline{ay}$(t) **ahl**vaa'lit
Can you repair it?	**Kan ni reparera det?**	kahn nee rehpahr**ay**rah d$\overline{ay}$(t)
Can you do it now?	**Kan ni göra det nu?**	kahn nee y$\overline{u}$rrah d$\overline{ay}$(t) new
What's it going to cost?	**Vad kommer det att kosta?**	vaa(d) **kom**merr d$\overline{ay}$(t) aht **kos**tah

What if he says "no"?

Why can't you do it?	**Varför kan ni inte göra det?**	**vah**rfurr kahn nee **in**ter y$\overline{u}$rrah d$\overline{ay}$(t)

Is it essential to have that part?	**Är den delen nöd-vändig?**	ær dehn **day**lern **nurd-**vehndi(g)
How long is it going to take to get the spare parts?	**Hur lång tid tar det att få reservdelen?**	hewr long teed taar **day**(t) aht foa rehss**ærv**day-lern
Where's the nearest garage that can repair it?	**Var ligger när-maste verkstad som kan laga det?**	vaar liggerr **nær-**mahster **værk**staa(d) som kahn **laa**gah **day**(t)
Can you fix it so that I can get as far as...?	**Kan ni bara laga det så pass att jag kan köra till...?**	kahn nee **baa**rah **laa**gah **day**(t) so pahss aht yaa(g) kahn **khur**rah til

If you're really stuck, ask:

| Can I leave my car here for a day/a few days? | **Kan jag lämna bilen här en dag/ett par dagar?** | kahn yaa(g) **lehm**nah **bee**lern hær ehn daag/eht paar **daa**(gah)r |

Settling the bill

Is everything fixed?	**Är allt lagat?**	ær ahlt **laa**gaht
How much do I owe you?	**Hur mycket blir jag skyldig?**	hewr **mew**ker(t) bleer yaa(g) **shewl**di(g)
Will you take a traveller's cheque?	**Tar ni emot en resecheck?**	taar nee eh**moot** ehn **ray**sserkhehk
Thanks very much for your help.	**Tack så mycket för hjälpen.**	tahk so **mew**ker(t) furr **yehl**pern
This is for you.	**Det här är för er.**	day(t) hær ær furr **ayr**

But you may feel that the workmanship is sloppy or that you're paying for work not done. Get the bill itemized. If necessary, get it translated before you pay.

| I'd like to check the bill first. Will you itemize the work done? | **Jag skulle vilja kontrollera räkningen först. Skulle ni kunna specificera den?** | yaa(g) **skew**ler **vil**yah kontroll**ay**rah **raik**ningern fur{sup}r{/sup}st. **skew**ler nee **kew**nah spehssiffiss**ay**rah dehn |

If the garage still won't back down, and you're sure you're right, get the help of a third party.

Some international road signs

No vehicles

No entry

No overtaking (passing)

Oncoming traffic has priority

Maximum speed limit

No parking

Caution

Intersection

Dangerous bend (curve)

Road narrows

Intersection with secondary road

Two-way traffic

Dangerous hill

Uneven road

Falling rocks

Give way (yield)

Main road,
thoroughfare

End of restriction

One-way traffic

Traffic goes
this way

Roundabout
(rotary)

Bicycles only

Pedestrians
only

Minimum speed
limit

Keep right
(left if symbol
reversed)

Parking

Hospital

Motorway
(expressway)

Motor vehicles
only

Filling station

No through road

Doctor

Frankly, how much use is a phrase book going to be to you in case of serious injury or illness? The only phrase you need in such an emergency is…

Get a doctor, quick!	**Skaffa genast en doktor!**	skahfah yāynahst ehn doktor

But there are minor aches and pains, ailments and irritations that can upset the best-planned trip. Here we can help you and, perhaps, the doctor.

Some doctors will speak English well; others will know enough for your needs. But suppose there's something the doctor can't explain because of language difficulties? We've thought of that. As you'll see, this section has been arranged to enable you and the doctor to communicate. From page 165 to 171, you'll find your part of the dialogue on the upper half of each page—the doctor's is on the lower half.

The whole section has been divided into three parts: illness, wounds, nervous tension. Page 171 is concerned with prescriptions and fees.

General

I need a doctor.	**Jag behöver en doktor.**	yaa(g) berhūrverr ehn doktor
Can you get me a doctor?	**Skulle ni kunna skaffa mig en doktor?**	skewler nee kewnah skahfah may ehn doktor
Is there a doctor here?	**Finns det någon doktor här?**	finss dāy(t) noagon doktor hæer
Please telephone for a doctor immediately.	**Var snäll och ring genast efter en doktor.**	vaar snehl ok ring yāynahst ehfterr ehn doktor
Where's there a doctor who speaks English?	**Var finns det en doktor som talar engelska?**	vaar finss dāy(t) ehn doktor som taalahr ehngerlskah

FOR CHEMISTS, see page 108

Where's the surgery (doctor's office)?	**Var ligger mottagningen?**	vaar ligger m$\overline{oo}$taagningern
What are the surgery (office) hours?	**Vilka är mottagningstiderna?**	vilkah ær m$\overline{oo}$taagningsteeder^{r}nah
Could the doctor come to see me here?	**Skulle doktorn kunna komma hit och undersöka mig?**	skewler dokto^{r}n kewnah kommah heet ok ewnder^{r}s$\overline{u}$rkah may
What time can the doctor come?	**Hur dags kan doktorn komma?**	h$\overline{ew}$r dahgss kahn dokto^{r}n kommah

Symptoms

Use this section to tell the doctor what's wrong. Basically, what he'll need to know is:

What?   (ache, pain, bruise etc.)
Where?   (arm, stomach etc.)
How long?   (have you had the trouble)

Before you visit the doctor find out the answers to these questions by glancing through the pages that follow. In this way, you'll save time.

Parts of the body

ankle	**vrist**	vrist
appendix	**blindtarm**	blin(d)tahrm
arm	**arm**	ahrm
artery	**artär**	ah^{r}tær
back	**rygg**	rewg
bladder	**urinblåsa**	ewreenbloassah
blood	**blod**	bl$\overline{oo}$d
bone	**ben (i kroppen)**	b$\overline{ay}$n (ee krohpern)
breast	**bröst**	brurst
cheek	**kind**	khind
chest	**bröstkorg**	brurstkory
chin	**haka**	haakah
ear	**öra**	$\overline{ur}$rah
elbow	**armbåge**	ahrmboager
eye	**öga**	$\overline{ur}$gah

DOCTOR

face	ansikte	ahnsikter
finger	finger	fingerr
foot	fot	fōōt
gall-bladder	gallblåsa	gahlbloassah
gland	körtel	khurtehl
hair	hår	hoar
hand	hand	hahnd
head	huvud	hēwvewd
heart	hjärta	yærtah
heel	häl	hail
hip	höft	hurft
intestines	tarmar	tahrmahr
jaw	käke	khaiker
joint	led	lāyd
kidney	njure	nyēwrer
knee	knä	knai
knuckle	knoge	knōōger
leg	ben	bāyn
ligament	ligament	liggahmehnt
lip	läpp	lehp
liver	lever	lāyverr
lung	lunga	lewngah
mouth	mun	mewn
muscle	muskel	mewskerl
neck	nacke	nahker
nerve	nerv	nærv
nervous system	nervsystemet	nærvsewstāymert
nose	näsa	naissah
pelvis	bäcken	behkern
rectum	ändtarm	ehndtahrm
rib	revben	rāyvbāyn
shoulder	axel	ahkserl
sinus	pannhåla	pahnhoalah
skin	hud	hēwd
spine	ryggrad	rewgraad
stomach	mage, magsäck	maager, maagsehk
tendon	sena	sāynah
thigh	lår	loar
throat	hals	hahlss
thumb	tumme	tewmer
toe	tå	toa
tongue	tunga	tewngah
tonsils	mandlar	mahndlahr
urine	urin	ewreen
vein	åder	oaderr
wrist	handled	hahn(d)lāyd

PATIENT

Part 1—Illness

I'm not feeling well.	**Jag känner mig inte bra.**	yaa(g) **kheh**nerr may **in**ter braa
I've got a pain here.	**Jag har ont här.**	yaa(g) haar oont hær
My/His/Her... hurts.	**Mitt/hans/ hennes... gör ont.**	mit/hahnss/**heh**nerss... yūrr oont
I've/He's/She's got (a)...	**Jag/han/hon har...**	yaa(g)/hahn/hon haar
backache	ont i ryggen	oont ee **rew**gern
fever	feber	**fay**berr
headache	huvudvärk	**hew**vewdværk
sore throat	ont i halsen	oont ee **hahls**sern
stomach ache	ont i magen	oont ee **maa**gern
I'm constipated.	**Jag har förstoppning.**	yaa(g) haar fur**'stop**ning
I've a bad cough.	**Jag har svår hosta.**	yaa(g) haar svoar **hoos**tah
I've been vomiting.	**Jag har kastat upp.**	yaa(g) haar **kahs**taht ewp

DOCTOR

DOCTOR

Del 1—Sjukdomar

Vad är det för fel?	What's the trouble?
Var gör det ont?	Where does it hurt?
Vad för slags smärta är det?	What sort of pain is it?
dov/intensiv/pulserande konstant/kommer och går	dull/sharp/throbbing constant/on and off
Hur länge har ni haft ont?	How long have you had this pain?
Hur länge har ni känt er så här?	How long have you been feeling like this?
Kavla upp ärmen.	Roll up your sleeve.
Var snäll och ta av er till midjan.	Please undress to the waist.

PATIENT

I feel...	Jag känner mig...	yaa(g) **kheh**nerr may
faint	**matt**	maht
dizzy	**yr**	ewr
nauseous	**illamående**	illahmoarnder
feverish	**febrig**	**fay**bri(g)
I've/He's/She's got (a/an)...	**Jag/han/hon har...**	yaa(g)/hahn/hon haar
abscess	**en varbildning**	ehn **vaar**bildning
asthma	**astma**	**ahst**mah
boil	**en böld**	ehn burld
chill	**blivit kall**	**blee**vit kahl
cold	**en förkylning**	ehn fur**khewl**ning
constipation	**förstoppning**	fur**r**stopning
cramps	**kramp**	krahmp
diarrhoea	**diarré**	diah**ray**
fever	**feber**	**fay**berr
hæmorrhoids	**hemorrojder**	hehmorruryderr
hay fever	**hösnuva**	**hur**snewvah
hernia	**bråck**	brok
indigestion	**dålig matsmält-ning**	**doa**li(g) **maat**smehltning
inflammation of...	**en...inflammation**	ehn...inflahmah**shoon**

DOCTOR

Var snäll och lägg er här.	Please lie down over here.
Öppna munnen.	Open your mouth.
Andas djupt.	Breathe deeply.
Hosta.	Cough, please.
Gör det här ont?	Does this hurt?
Jag skall ta er temperatur.	I'll take your temperature.
Är det första gången ni har det här?	Is this the first time you've had this?
Jag vill ha ett urinprov/ avföringsprov.	I want a sample of your urine/ stools.
Vilken blodgrupp har ni?	What is your blood type?

PATIENT

influenza	**influensa**	inflewehnssah
measles	**mässling**	mehsling
morning sickness	**kväljningar på morgonen**	kvehlyningahr poa morronnern
rheumatism	**reumatism**	rehmahtissm
stiff neck	**stel nacke**	stāyl nahker
sunburn	**solsveda**	sōōlssvāydah
sunstroke	**solsting**	sōōlssting
tonsillitis	**halsfluss**	hahlssflewss
ulcer	**magsår**	maagssoar
whooping cough	**kikhosta**	kheekhoosstah
It's nothing serious I hope?	**Det är ingenting allvarligt, hoppas jag?**	dāy(t) ǣr ingernting ahlvaa'lit hoppahss yaa(g)
I'd like you to prescribe some medicine for me.	**Skulle ni kunna skriva ut lite medicin?**	skewler nee kewnnah skreevah ēwt leeter mehdersseen

DOCTOR

Det är ingenting att oroa sig för.	It's nothing to worry about.
Ni måste ligga till sängs i... dagar.	You must stay in bed for... days.
Ni har...	You've got (a/an)...
blindtarmsinflammation	appendicitis
ledinflammation	arthritis
förkylning	cold
matförgiftning	food poisoning
inflammation i...	inflammation of...
influensa/magsår	influenza/ulcer
Ni är överansträngd. Ni behöver vila.	You're over-tired. You need a rest.
Jag tycker att ni skall vända er till en specialist.	I want you to see a specialist.
Jag tycker ni skall göra en allmän undersökning på sjukhuset.	I want you to go to the hospital for a general check-up.
Jag skall skriva ut antibiotika.	I'll prescribe an antibiotic.

DOCTOR

PATIENT

I'm a diabetic.	**Jag är diabetiker.**	yaa(g) ær diahbaytikkerr
I've a cardiac condition.	**Jag har hjärtfel.**	yaa(g) haar yæⁱtfayl
I had a heart attack in...	**Jag hade en hjärt-attack i...**	yaa(g) hahder ehn yæⁱtahtahk ee
I'm allergic to...	**Jag är allergisk mot...**	yaa(g) ær ahlærgisk moot
This is my usual medicine.	**Jag brukar ta den här medicinen.**	yaa(g) brewkahr taa dehn hær mehdersseenern
I need this medicine.	**Jag behöver den här medicinen.**	yaa(g) berhürverr dehn hær mehdersseenern
I'm expecting a baby.	**Jag väntar barn.**	yaa(g) vehntahr baaⁱn
Can I travel?	**Kan jag resa?**	kahn yaa(g) rayssah

DOCTOR

Hur stor mängd insulin tar ni?	What dose of insulin are you taking?
Intravenöst eller genom munnen?	Injection or oral?
Vilken behandling har ni fått?	What treatment have you been having?
Vilken medicin har ni tagit?	What medicine have you been taking?
Tål ni penicillin?	Have you ever had ill effects from penicillin?
Ni har haft en (lätt) hjärtattack.	You've had a (slight) heart attack.
Vi har inte...i Sverige. Det här är nästan likadant.	We don't use... in Sweden. This is very similar.
När väntas nedkomsten?	When's the baby due?
Ni kan inte resa förrän...	You can't travel until...

PATIENT

Part 2—Wounds

Could you have a look at this...?	Skulle ni kunna undersöka...	skewler nee kewnah ewnder^{r}ssurkah
blister	blåsan	bloassahn
boil	bölden	burldern
bruise	blåmärket	bloamærkert
burn	brännsåret	brehnssoarert
cut	skärsåret	shæ^{r}ssoarert
graze	skrubbsåret	skrewbssoarert
insect bite	insektsbettet	insehktsbehtert
lump	knölen	knurlern
rash	rodnaden	roadnahdern
swelling	svullnaden	svewlnahdern
wound	såret	soarert
I can't move my...	Jag kan inte röra...	yaa(g) kahn inter rurrah
It hurts.	Det gör ont.	day(t) yurr oont

DOCTOR

Del 2—Skador, sår

Det är (inte) infekterat.	It's (not) infected.
Ni har en kotförskjutning.	You've got a slipped disc.
Jag tycker ni skall röntga det.	I want you to have an x-ray.
Har ni vaccinerats mot stelkramp? När?	Have you been vaccinated against tetanus? When?
Det är...	It's...
brutet/vrickat ur led/stukat	broken/sprained dislocated/torn
Ni har sträckt en muskel.	You've pulled a muscle.
Jag skall ge er lite anti-septisk salva.	I'll give you an antiseptic.
Det är inte allvarligt.	It's not serious.
Låt mig få se på det igen om...dagar.	I want you to come and see me in...days' time.

DOCTOR

PATIENT

Part 3—Nervous tension

I'm in a nervous state.	**Jag är nervös.**	yaa(g) ǟr nehrv**ūrss**
I'm feeling depressed.	**Jag känner mig deprimerad.**	yaa(g) khehnerr may dehprimm**ay**rahd
I want some sleeping pills.	**Jag skulle vilja ha några sömn-tabletter.**	yaa(g) **skew**ler vil**y**ah haa **noa**grah surmntah-blehterr
I can't eat.	**Jag kan inte äta.**	yaa(g) kahn **inter** aitah
I can't sleep.	**Jag kan inte sova.**	yaa(g) kahn **inter soavah**
I'm having nightmares.	**Jag har mardrömmar.**	yaa(g) haar **maardrurmahr**
Can you prescribe a...?	**Kan ni skriva ut...?**	kahn nee **skreevah ēwt**
tranquillizer anti-depressant	**ett lugnande medel någonting mot depression**	eht **lewng**nahnder **may**derl **noa**gonting mōōt dehprer**shōōn**

DOCTOR

Del 3—Nervösa besvär

Ni är nervös och spänd.	You're suffering from nervous tension.
Ni behöver vila.	You need a rest.
Vilken medicin har ni tagit?	What medicine have you been taking?
Hur många om dagen?	How many a day?
Hur länge har ni känt er så här?	How long have you been feeling like this?
Jag skall skriva ut lite medicin.	I'll prescribe some medicine.
Jag skall ge er ett lugnande medel.	I'll give you a tranquillizer.

PATIENT

Prescriptions and dosage

What kind of medicine is this?	Vad för slags medicin är det här?	vaa(d) fūrr slahgss mehdersseen ǟr dāy(t) hǟr
How many times a day should I take it?	Hur många gånger om dagen bör jag ta den?	hēwr mongah gongerr om daa(ger)n būrr yaa(g) taa dehn
Must I swallow them whole?	Måste jag svälja dem hela?	moster yaa(g) svehlyah dehm hāylah

Fee

How much do I owe you?	Hur mycket blir jag skyldig?	hēwr mewker(t) bleer yaa(g) shewldi(g)
Do I pay you now or will you send me your bill?	Skall jag betala er nu eller skickar ni räkningen?	skahl yaa(g) bertaalah ǟyr nēw ehler shikkahr nee raikningern
May I have a receipt?	Kan jag få ett kvitto?	kahn yaa(g) foa eht kvitto

DOCTOR

Recept och dosering

Ta...teskedar av den här medicinen var...timme.	Take...teaspoons of this medicine every...hours.
Ta...piller med ett glas vatten...	Take...pills with a glass of water...
...gånger om dagen	...times a day
före varje måltid	before each meal
efter varje måltid	after each meal
på morgonen/på kvällen	in the mornings/at night

Arvode

Var snäll och betala mig nu.	Please pay me now.
Jag skickar er räkningen.	I'll send you a bill.

FOR NUMBERS, see page 175

DOCTOR

Dentist

Can you recommend a good dentist?	**Kan ni föreslå en bra tandläkare?**	kahn nee fürrersloa ehn braa **tahn(d)**laikahrer
Can I make an (urgent) appointment to see Doctor...?	**Kan jag få tid (så snart som möjligt) hos doktor...?**	kahn yaa(g) foa teed (soa snaaᵉt som murylit) hooss **doktor**
I've got toothache.	**Jag har tandvärk.**	yaa(g) haar **tahn(d)**værk
I've an abscess.	**Jag har varbild-ning.**	yaa(g) haar **vaar**bildning
This tooth hurts.	**Den här tanden gör ont.**	dehn hær **tahn**dern yürr oont
at the top	**där uppe**	dær **ew**per
at the bottom	**där nere**	dær **nay**rer
in the front	**där fram**	dær frahm
at the back	**där bak**	dær baak
Can you fix it temporarily?	**Kan ni göra en pro-visorisk lagning?**	kahn nee **yürr**ah ehn proovis**sōō**risk **laag**ning
I don't want it extracted.	**Jag vill inte få den utdragen.**	yaa(g) vil inter foa dehn **ew**tdraagern
I've a loose tooth.	**Jag har en lös tand.**	yaa(g) haar ehn lȳrss tahnd
I've broken a tooth.	**Jag har brutit av en tand.**	yaa(g) haar **brew**tit aav ehn tahnd
I've lost a filling.	**Jag har tappat en plomb.**	yaa(g) haar **tah**paht ehn plomb
The gum is very sore.	**Tandköttet gör mycket ont.**	**tahn(d)**khurtert yürr **mew**ker(t) oont
The gum is bleeding.	**Tandköttet blöder.**	**tahn(d)**khurtert **blȳ**derr

Dentures

I've broken this denture.	**Jag har slagit sönder den här tandprotesen.**	yaa(g) haar **slaa**git **surn**derr dehn hær **tahn(d)**prootāyssern
Can you repair this denture?	**Skulle ni kunna laga den här tand-protesen?**	**skew**ler nee **kew**nah **laa**gah dehn hær **tahn(d)**prootāyssern
When will it be ready?	**När blir det klart?**	nær bleer dāy(t) klaaᵉt

Optician

I've broken my glasses.	**Jag har slagit sönder mina glasögon.**	yaa(g) haar **slaa**git **surn**derr **mee**nah **glaass**ū̄rgon
Can you repair them for me?	**Kan ni laga dem åt mig?**	kahn nee **laa**gah dehm oat may
When will they be ready?	**När blir de klara?**	nær bleer deh **klaa**rah
Can you change the lenses?	**Kan ni byta ut glasen?**	kahn nee **bew**tah ēwt **glaass**ern
I've lost one of my contact lenses.	**Jag har tappat en av mina kontaktlinser.**	yaa(g) haar **tah**paht ehn aav **mee**nah kon**tahkt**linsserr
I'd like to buy a pair of binoculars.	**Jag skulle vilja köpa en kikare.**	yaa(g) **skew**ler **vil**yah **khū̄**pah ehn **khee**kahrer
I'd like to buy a pair of sun-glasses.	**Jag skulle vilja köpa ett par solglasögon.**	yaa(g) **skew**ler **vil**yah **khū̄**pah eht paar **sool**glaass**ū̄**rgon
How much do I owe you?	**Hur mycket blir jag skyldig?**	hēwr **mew**ker(t) bleer yaa(g) **shewl**di(g)
Do I pay you now or will you send me your bill?	**Skall jag betala er nu eller skickar ni räkningen?**	skahl yaa(g) ber**taa**lah ā̄yr nēw **eh**lerr **shi**kkahr nee **raik**ningern

Keeping fit

Your hotel or the local tourist office can help you find a gymnasium or health institute to keep you physically fit away from home or tone up those tired muscles.

Where can I find a...?	**Var finner jag...?**	vaar **finn**err yaa(g)
massage parlour	**ett massageinstitut**	eht mah**ssash**institt**ēw**t
physiotherapist	**en sjukgymnast**	ehn **shēw**kyewmnahst
sauna	**en bastu**	ehn **bah**stew
solarium	**ett solarium**	eht **soo**lahriewm
Turkish bath	**ett turkiskt bad**	eht **tur**kiskt baad
Where can I find a gymnasium. I want to work out.	**Var finner jag en gymnastiksal. Jag behöver motion.**	vaar **finn**err yaa(g) ehn gewmnah**steeks**saal. yaa(g) ber**hū̄**verr mot**shoon**

FOR NUMBERS, see page 175

Reference section

Where do you come from?

Or, "we're from…", "we're going to…next", "what does a postcard to…cost?" The names of some countries sound very similar in Swedish and in English, but there are others your listener wouldn't understand at all if you pronounced them the English way. The following list of countries will help you over this problem.

Africa	**Afrika**	aafrikkah
Asia	**Asien**	aassiern
Australia	**Australien**	aaewstraaliern
China	**Kina**	kheenah
Denmark	**Danmark**	dahnmahrk
England	**England**	ehnglahnd
Europe	**Europa**	ehewrōōpah
Finland	**Finland**	finlahnd
France	**Frankrike**	frahnkrikker
Germany	**Tyskland**	tewsklahnd
Great Britain	**Storbritannien**	stōōrbrittahniern
India	**Indien**	indiern
Ireland	**Irland**	irlahnd
Japan	**Japan**	yaapahn
New Zealand	**Nya Zeeland**	nēwah sāylahnd
North America	**Nordamerika**	noorʳdahmāyrikkah
Norway	**Norge**	noryer
Scandinavia	**Skandinavien**	skahndinnaaviern
Scotland	**Skottland**	skotlahnd
South Africa	**Sydafrika**	sēwdaafrikkah
South America	**Sydamerika**	sēwdahmāyrikkah
Sweden	**Sverige**	svehryer
USA	**USA**	ēwehssah
USSR	**Sovjetunionen**	sovyehtewniōōnern
Wales	**Wales**	wayless

Numbers

0	noll	nol
1	ett	eht
2	två	tvoa
3	tre	trāy
4	fyra	fewrah
5	fem	fehm
6	sex	sehks
7	sju	shew
8	åtta	ottah
9	nio	neeoo
10	tio	teeoo
11	elva	ehlvah
12	tolv	tolv
13	tretton	trehton
14	fjorton	fyoorton
15	femton	fehmton
16	sexton	sehkston
17	sjutton	shewton
18	arton	ahrton
19	nitton	nitton
20	tjugo	khewgoo
21	tjugoett	khewgoeht
22	tjugotvå	khewgotvoa
23	tjugotre	khewgotrāy
24	tjugofyra	khewgofewrah
25	tjugofem	khewgofehm
26	tjugosex	khewgossehks
27	tjugosju	khewgosshew
28	tjugoåtta	khewgoottah
29	tjugonio	khewgoneeoo
30	trettio	threhti
31	trettioett	trehtieht
32	trettiotvå	trehtitvoa
33	trettiotre	trehtitrāy
40	fyrtio	furrti
41	fyrtioett	furrtieht
42	fyrtiotvå	furrtitvoa
43	fyrtiotre	furrtitrāy
50	femtio	fehmti
51	femtioett	fehmtieht
52	femtiotvå	fehmtitvoa
53	femtiotre	fehmtitrāy
60	sextio	sehksti
61	sextioett	sehkstieht

62	sextiotvå	sehkstitvoa
63	sextiotre	sehkstitrāy
70	sjuttio	shewti
71	sjuttioett	shewtieht
72	sjuttiotvå	shewtitvoa
73	sjuttiotre	shewtitrāy
80	åttio	otti
81	åttioett	ottieht
82	åttiotvå	ottitvoa
83	åttiotre	ottitrāy
90	nittio	nitti
91	nittioett	nittieht
92	nittiotvå	nittitvoa
93	nittiotre	nittitrāy
100	(ett)hundra	(eht)hewndrah
101	hundraett	hewndraheht
102	hundratvå	hewndrahtvoa
110	hundratio	hewndrahteeoo
120	hundratjugo	hewndrahkhēwgoo
130	hundratrettio	hewndrahtrehti
140	hundrafyrtio	hewndrahfurᶦti
150	hundrafemtio	hewndrahfehmti
160	hundrasextio	hewndrahssehksti
170	hundrasjuttio	hewndrahshewti
180	hundraåttio	hewndrahotti
190	hundranittio	hewndrahnitti
200	tvåhundra	tvoahewndrah
300	trehundra	trāyhewndrah
400	fyrahundra	fēwrahhewndrah
500	femhundra	fehmhewndrah
600	sexhundra	sehkshewndrah
700	sjuhundra	shēwhewndrah
800	åttahundra	ottahewndrah
900	niohundra	neeoohewndrah
1000	(ett) tusen	(eht) tēwssern
1100	ettusenetthundra	ehtēwssernehthewndrah
	(elvahundra)	(ehlvahhewndrah)
1200	ettusentvåhundra	ehtēwsserntvoahewndrah
	(tolvhundra)	(tolvhewndrah)
2000	tvåtusen	tvoatēwssern
5000	femtusen	fehmtēwssern
10,000	tiotusen	teeootēwssern
50,000	femtiotusen	fehmtittēwssern
100,000	(ett)hundratusen	(eht)hewndrahtewssern
1,000,000	en miljon	ehn milyōōn
1,000,000,000	en miljard	ehn milyaaᶦd

first	**första**	fur^rstah
second	**andra**	ahndrah
third	**tredje**	trāȳdyer
fourth	**fjärde**	fyǣ^rder
fifth	**femte**	fehmter
sixth	**sjätte**	shehter
seventh	**sjunde**	shewnder
eighth	**åttonde**	ottonder
ninth	**nionde**	neeoonder
tenth	**tionde**	teeoonder
once	**en gång**	ehn gong
twice	**två gånger**	tvoa gongerr
three times	**tre gånger**	trāȳ gongerr
a half	**en halv**	ehn hahlv
half of...	**hälften av**	hehlftern aav
half a...	**halva**	hahlvah
a quarter	**en kvart**	ehn kvah^rt
three-quarters	**tre kvart**	trāȳ kvah^rt
a third	**en tredjedel**	ehn **trāȳ**dyerdāȳl
two-thirds	**två tredjedelar**	tvoa **trāȳ**dyerdāȳlahr
a pair of	**ett par**	eht paar
a dozen	**ett dussin**	eht dewssin
1985	**nittonhundra-åttiofem**	nittonhewndrah-otti**fehm**
1987	**nittonhundra-åttiosju**	nittonhewndrah-otti**shew**
1990	**nittonhundra-nittio**	nittonhewndrah-**nitti**

Time

kvart över tolv
(kvah^rt ūrverr tolv)

tjugo över ett
(khewgo ūrverr eht)

fem i halv tre
(fehm ee hahlv trāy)

halv fyra
(hahlv fewrah)

fem över halv fem
(fehm ūrverr hahlv fehm)

tjugo i sex
(khewgo ee sehks)

kvart i sju
(kvah^rt ee shew)

tio i åtta
(teeoo ee ottah)

fem i nio
(fehm ee neeoo)

tio
(teeoo)

fem över elva
(fehm ūrverr ehlvah)

tio över tolv
(teeoo ūrverr tolv)

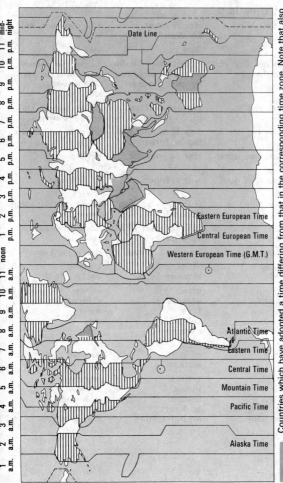

a.m. 1 / 2 a.m. / 3 a.m. / 4 a.m. / 5 a.m. / 6 a.m. / 7 a.m. / 8 a.m. / 9 a.m. / 10 a.m. / 11 a.m. / noon / 1 p.m. / 2 p.m. / 3 p.m. / 4 p.m. / 5 p.m. / 6 p.m. / 7 p.m. / 8 p.m. / 9 p.m. / 10 p.m. / 11 p.m. / midnight

Date Line

Eastern European Time

Central European Time

Western European Time (G.M.T.)

Atlantic Time

Eastern Time

Central Time

Mountain Time

Pacific Time

Alaska Time

REFERENCE SECTION

Countries which have adopted a time differing from that in the corresponding time zone. Note that also in the USSR, official time is one hour ahead of the time in each corresponding time zone. In summer, numerous countries advance time one hour ahead of standard time.

What time is it?

What time is it?	**Hur mycket är klockan?**	hewr mewker(t) ær klokkahn
It's...	**Den är...**	dehn ær
Excuse me. Can you tell me the time?	**Förlåt mig. Skulle ni kunna säga hur mycket klockan är?**	fur'loat may. skewler nee kewnah sehyah hewr mewker(t) klokkahn ær
I'll meet you at... tomorrow.	**Låt oss träffas kl... i morgon.**	loat oss trehfass klokkahn...ee morron
I'm sorry I'm late.	**Jag är ledsen att jag är försenad.**	yaa(g) ær lehssern aht yaa(g) ær furrsaÿnahd
At what time does... open?	**När öppnar...?**	nær urpnahr
At what time does... close?	**När stänger...?**	nær stehngerr
At what time should I be there?	**Hur dags bör jag vara där?**	hewr dahgss burr yaa(g) vaarah dær
At what time will you be there?	**När kommer ni att vara där?**	nær kommerr nee aht vaarah dær
Can I come...?	**Kan jag komma...?**	kahn yaa(g) kommah
at 8 o'clock	**klockan 8**	klokkahn 8
at 2.30	**klockan 14.30**	klokkahn 14.30
after (prep.)	**efter**	ehfterr
afterwards	**efteråt**	ehfterroat
before	**före**	furrer
early	**tidigt**	teedit
in time	**i tid**	ee teed
late	**sent**	saÿnt
midnight	**midnatt**	meednaht
noon	**klockan 12**	klokkahn 12
hour	**timme**	teemmer
minute	**minut**	meenewt
second	**sekund**	sehkewndh
quarter of an hour	**en kvart**	ehn kvah'rt
half an hour	**en halvtimme**	ehn hahlvtimmer

Days

What day is it today?	**Vad är det för dag idag?**	vaa(d) ǣr dāy(t) fūrr daag iddaa(g)
Sunday	**söndag**	surndaa(g)
Monday	**måndag**	mondaa(g)
Tuesday	**tisdag**	teesdaa(g)
Wednesday	**onsdag**	oonsdaa(g)
Thursday	**torsdag**	toorsdaa(g)
Friday	**fredag**	frāydaa(g)
Saturday	**lördag**	lurrdaa(g)
in the morning	**på morgonen**	poa morronnern
during the day	**under dagen**	ewnderr daagern
in the afternoon	**på eftermiddagen**	poa ehfterrmiddaagern
in the evening	**på kvällen**	poa kvehlern
at night	**på natten**	poa nahtern
the day before yesterday	**i förrgår**	ee furrgoar
yesterday	**igår**	iggoar
today	**idag**	iddaa(g)
tomorrow	**i morgon**	ee morron
the day after tomorrow	**i övermorgon**	ee ūverrmorron
the day before	**dagen före**	daa(ger)n fūrrer
the following day	**dagen efter**	daa(ger)n ehfterr
two days ago	**för två dagar sedan**	fūrr tvoa daa(gah)r sāydahn
in three days' time	**om tre dagar**	om trāy daa(gah)r
last week	**förra veckan**	furrah vehkahn
next week	**nästa vecka**	nehstah vehkah
for a fortnight (two weeks)	**i två veckor**	ee tvoa vehkoor
birthday	**födelsedag**	fūrdehlserdaa(g)
day	**dag**	daag
day off	**ledig dag**	lāydi(g) daag
holiday	**helgdag**	hehlydaa(g)
holidays	**semester**	sehmehsterr
month	**månad**	moanahd
school holidays	**skollov**	skooloov
vacation	**semester**	sehmehsterr
week	**vecka**	vehkah
weekday	**veckodag**	vehkodaa(g)
weekend	**helg (veckända)**	hehly (vehkehndah)
working day	**arbetsdag**	ahrbehtsdaa(g)

Months

January	**januari**	yahnewaari
February	**februari**	fehbrewaari
March	**mars**	mahʳss
April	**april**	ahpril
May	**maj**	may
June	**juni**	yēwni
July	**juli**	yēwli
August	**augusti**	ahgewsti
September	**september**	sehptehmberr
October	**oktober**	ooktōoberr
November	**november**	noovehmberr
December	**december**	derssehmberr
since June	**sedan juni**	sāydahn yēwni
during the month of August	**under augusti månad**	ewnderr ahgewsti moanahd
last month	**förra månaden**	furrah moanahdern
next month	**nästa månad**	nehstah moanahd
the month before	**månaden före**	moanahdern fürrer
the following month	**följande månad**	furlyahnder moanahd
July 1	**första juli**	furʳstah yēwli
March 17	**sjuttonde mars**	shewtonder mahʳss

Letter headings are written as follows:

> **Stockholm, July 1, 19. .**   Stockholm, den 1 juli 19. .
> **Gothenburg, March 17, 19. .**   Göteborg, den 17 mars 19. .

Seasons

spring	**vår**	voar
summer	**sommar**	sommahr
autumn	**höst**	hurst
winter	**vinter**	vinterr
in spring	**på våren**	poa voarern
during the summer	**under sommaren**	ewnderr sommahrern
last autumn	**förra hösten**	furrah hurstern
next winter	**nästa vinter**	nehstah vinterr

Public holidays

Note that on the days before most public holidays offices, banks, post offices and shops usually observe shorter, Saturday working hours.

January 1	**Nyårsdagen**	New Year's Day
January 6	**Trettondagen**	Epiphany
May 1	**Första Maj**	May Day
On the Saturday that falls between June 20 and 26	**Midsommardagen**	Midsummer Day
On the Saturday that falls between October 31 and November 6	**Allhelgonadagen**	All Saints' Day
December 25/26	**Juldagen/Annandag jul**	Christmas Day/Boxing Day
Movable dates:	**Långfredagen**	Good Friday
	Påskdagen/Annandag påsk	Easter/Easter Monday
	Kristi himmelsfärdsdag	Ascension
	Pingstdagen/Annandag pingst	Whit-Sunday/Monday

The year round...

Here are the average temperatures for some cities in centigrade:

	Gothenburg	Stockholm	Östersund	Haparanda
January	− 1.1	− 2.9	− 8.4	−10.6
April	+ 5.6	+ 4.4	+ 1.2	− 0.9
July	+17.0	+17.8	+14.7	+16.3
October	+ 8.8	+ 7.1	+ 3.8	+ 2.1

Common abbreviations

Here are some Swedish abbreviations you're likely to encounter:

AB	**aktiebolag**	Ltd.
av.	**aveny**	avenue
avd.	**avdelning**	department
bl.a.	**bland annat**	among others
Co.	**kompani**	company
D	**Damer**	Ladies
e.m.	**eftermiddag**	p.m.
f.m.	**förmiddag**	a.m.
Frk	**fröken**	Miss
g.	**gata**	street
g	**gram**	grams
H	**Herrar**	Gentlemen
Hr	**herr**	Mr.
KAK	**Kungliga Automobil-klubben**	Royal Automobile Club
kg	**kilogram**	kilograms
kl.	**klockan**	o'clock
km	**kilometer**	kilometres
kr.	**kronor**	crowns
l	**liter**	litres
m	**meter**	metres
moms	**mervärdeskatt**	value added tax
nr	**nummer**	number
n.b.	**nedre botten**	ground floor
osv.	**och så vidare**	etc.
SJ	**Statens Järnvägar**	Swedish State Railways
STF	**Svenska Turistför-eningen**	Swedish Tourist Office
STTF	**Svenska Turisttrafik-föreningen**	Swedish Tourist Transport Association
tr.	**trappor**	stairs
UD	**Utrikes-departementet**	Ministry for Foreign Affairs
v.	**vägen**	road

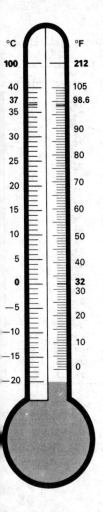

Conversion tables

Centimetres and inches

To change centimetres into inches, multiply by .39.

To change inches into centimetres, multiply by 2.54.

	in.	feet	yards
1 mm	0.039	0.003	0.001
1 cm	0.39	0.03	0.01
1 dm	3.94	0.32	0.10
1 m	39.40	3.28	1.09

	mm	cm	m
1 in.	25.4	2.54	0.025
1 ft.	304.8	30.48	0.305
1 yd.	914.4	91.44	0.914

(32 metres = 35 yards)

Temperature

To convert centigrade into degrees Fahrenheit, multiply centigrade by 1.8 and add 32.

To convert degrees Fahrenheit into centigrade, subtract 32 from Fahrenheit and divide by 1.8.

Metres and feet

The figure in the middle stands for both metres and feet, e.g.,
1 metre = 3.281 ft. and 1 foot = 0.30 m.

Metres		Feet
0.30	1	3.281
0.61	2	6.563
0.91	3	9.843
1.22	4	13.124
1.52	5	16.403
1.83	6	19.686
2.13	7	22.967
2.44	8	26.248
2.74	9	29.529
3.05	10	32.810
3.35	11	36.091
3.66	12	39.372
3.96	13	42.635
4.27	14	45.934
4.57	15	49.215
4.88	16	52.496
5.18	17	55.777
5.49	18	59.058
5.79	19	62.339
6.10	20	65.620
7.62	25	82.023
15.24	50	164.046
22.86	75	246.069
30.48	100	328.092

Other conversion charts

Weight conversion

The figure in the middle stands for both kilograms and pounds, e.g., 1 kilogram = 2.205 lb. and 1 pound = 0.45 kilograms.

Kilograms (kg.)		Avoirdupois pounds
0.45	1	2.205
0.90	2	4.405
1.35	3	6.614
1.80	4	8.818
2.25	5	11.023
2.70	6	13.227
3.15	7	15.432
3.60	8	17.636
4.05	9	19.840
4.50	10	22.045
6.75	15	33.068
9.00	20	44.889
11.25	25	55.113
22.50	50	110.225
33.75	75	165.338
45.00	100	220.450

REFERENCE SECTION

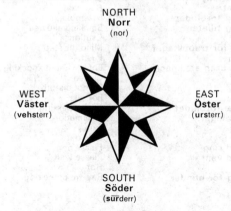

NORTH
Norr
(nor)

WEST
Väster
(**veh**sterr)

EAST
Öster
(**ur**sterr)

SOUTH
Söder
(**sūr**derr)

What does that sign mean?

You're sure to encounter some of these signs or notices on your trip:

Att hyra	To let, for hire
Cykelstig	Cycle path
Damer	Ladies
Drag	Pull
Fara	Danger
Fritt inträde	Admission free
Får ej vidröras	Do not touch
...förbjuden	...forbidden
Herrar	Gentlemen
Hiss	Lift (elevator)
Ingång	Entrance
Ingen ingång	No entry
Kallt	Cold
Kassa	Cashier's
Ledigt	Vacant
Livsfara	Danger of Death
Nödutgång	Emergency exit
Privat	Private
Privat väg	Private road
Rea(lisation)	Sales
Reservat	Reserved
Rökning förbjuden	No smoking
Rökning tillåten	Smoking allowed
Se upp	Caution
Se upp för trappsteget	Mind the step
Skjut	Push
Stig på utan att knacka	Enter without knocking
Stängt	Closed
Stör ej	Do not disturb
Till salu	For sale
Tillträde förbjudet	No trespassing
Upplysningar	Information
Utgång	Exit
Utsålt	Sold out
Var god ring	Please ring
Var god vänta	Please wait
Varmt	Hot
Varning för hunden	Beware of the dog

Emergency

By the time the emergency is upon you it's too late to turn to this page to find the Swedish for "I'll scream if you..." So have a look at this short list beforehand —and, if you want to be on the safe side, learn the expressions shown in capitals.

Be quick	**Gör det snabbt**	yŭrr dāy(t) snahbt
Call the police	**Ring efter polisen**	ring ehfterr poleessern
CAREFUL	**FÖRSIKTIGT**	furrsiktit
Come here	**Kom hit**	kom heet
Come in	**Kom in**	kom in
Danger	**Fara**	faarah
Fire	**Elden är lös**	ehldern ær lŭrss
Gas	**Gas**	gaass
Get a doctor	**Hämta en läkare**	hehmtah ehn laikahrer
Go away	**Ge er iväg**	yāy āyr ivvaig
HELP	**HJÄLP**	yehlp
Get help quickly	**Skaffa hjälp fort**	skahfah yehlp foort
I'm ill	**Jag är sjuk**	yaa(g) ær shēwk
I'm lost	**Jag har gått vilse**	yaa(g) haar got vilser
I've lost my...	**Jag har tappat mitt...**	yaa(g) haar tahpaht mit
Keep your hands to yourself	**Bort med fingrarna**	boort māyd fing-rahrnah
Leave me alone	**Låt mig vara ifred**	loat may vaarah ifrāyd
Lie down	**Ligg ner**	lig nāyr
Listen	**Hör på**	hŭrr poa
Listen to me	**Lyssna på mig**	lewsnah poa may
Look	**Titta**	tittah
LOOK OUT	**SE UPP**	sāy ewp
POLICE	**POLIS**	poleess
Quick	**Fort**	foort
STOP	**STOPP**	stop
Stop here	**Stanna här**	stahnah hær
Stop that man	**Stoppa den där mannen**	stoppah dehn dær mahnern
STOP THIEF	**STOPPA TJUVEN**	stoppah khēwvern
Stop or I'll scream	**Stanna annars skriker jag**	stahnah ahnahrs skreekerr yaa(g)

FOR CAR ACCIDENTS, see page 150

REFERENCE SECTION

Index

Quick reference page

Here are some phrases and expressions which you'll probably need most frequently on your trip:

Please.	**Var så god.**	vaar soa gōōd
Thank you.	**Tack.**	tahk
Yes/No.	**Ja/Nej.**	yaa/nay
Excuse me.	**Förlåt mig.**	fur^rloat may
Waiter, please.	**Hovmästaren!**	hoavmehstahrern
How much is that?	**Hur mycket blir det där?**	hēēr mewker(t) bleer dāy(t) dær
Where are the toilets?	**Var ligger toaletterna?**	vaar liggerr tooahleh-ter^rnah

Toaletter	
HERRAR	DAMER
hehrahr	daamerr

Could you tell me...?	**Skulle ni kunna säga mig...?**	skewler nee kewnah sehyah may
where/when/why	**var/när/varför**	vaar/nær/**vahr**furr
Help me, please.	**Var snäll och hjälp mig.**	vaar snehl ok yehlp may
What time is it?	**Vad är klockan?**	vaa(d) ær klokkahn
one/first	**en/första**	ehn/fur^rstah
two/second	**två/andra**	tvoa/**ahn**drah
three/third	**tre/tredje**	trāy/**trāy**dyer
What does this mean?	**Vad betyder det här?**	vaa(d) bertēwderr dāy(t) hær
I don't understand.	**Jag förstår inte.**	yaa(g) fur^rstoar inter
Do you speak English?	**Talar ni engelska?**	taalahr nee **ehng**erlskah